Enabled- Living God's Purpose With Power

Joshua Rhoades

Published by Joshua Paul Rhoades, 2024.

While every precaution has been taken in the preparation of this book, the publisher assumes no responsibility for errors or omissions, or for damages resulting from the use of the information contained herein.

ENABLED- LIVING GOD'S PURPOSE WITH POWER

First edition. November 8, 2024.

Copyright © 2024 Joshua Rhoades.

ISBN: 979-8224519293

Written by Joshua Rhoades.

Also by Joshua Rhoades

Courage Under Fire: David's Stand On The Battlefield
Jonah's Journey: Voices Of Redemption And Lessons In Obedience
The Furnace Of Faith: 12 Principles From The Heat Of Faith
Whispers of Hope: Inspiring Stories of Men's Prayers In Scripture
Frontier Legends: The Oregon Dream
Elijah: A Beacon Of Boldness
HOOK, LINE & SAVIOUR - Faith Reflections from Fishing
Driven By Faith: Motor Racing Inspired Christian Life
30 Day Devotional - Bold and Strong- Coffee Devotions for a Courageous Christian Walk
Authentic Christianity: The Heart of Old Time Religion
Consider The Ant - God's Tiny Preachers
Flee Fornication: The Plea For Purity
Renewed Hope- How to Find Encouragement in God
Sounding The Call - The Voice of Conviction
The Altar - Where Heaven Meets Earth
The Bible's Battlefields- Timeless Lessons from Ancient Wars
The Sacred Art of Silence - How Silence Speaks in Scripture
Under Fire- The Sanctity of the Traditional Biblical Home
Who Is on the Lord's Side? A Call to Righteousness
What Is Truth? - From Skepticism to Submission
First and Goal- Faith and Football Fundamentals
From Dugout to Devotion- Spiritual Lessons from Baseball
Par for the Course- Faith and Fairways
The Believer's Pace- Tools for Running Life's Marathon
The Immutable Fortress- Security in God's Unchanging Nature
Biblical Bravery
Deer Stands and Devotions: A Hunter's Walk with God

Jesus Knows- Our Hearts, Our Responsibility
Restoration - Setting The Bone
Spiritual 911- God's Word for Life's Emergency's
The Freedom of Forgiveness
The Jezebel Effect - Ancient Manipulations Modern Lessons
The Shout That Stopped The Saviour
The Time Machine Chronicles: Old Testament Characters
Anchored In Truth Exploring The Depths of Psalm 119
Biblical Counsel on Anger
Proverbs' Portraits The Men God Mentions
Stumbling in the Dark - The Dangers of Alcohol
Guarding the Wicket Protecting Your Faith and Game
The Champion's Faith - Wrestling and Achieving Spiritual Victory
Scriptural Commands for Modern Times Living God's Word Today Volume 1
Scriptural Commands for Modern Times Living God's Word Today Volume 2
Scriptural Commands for Modern Times Living God's Word TodayVolume3
The Greatest Gift
A Christmas Journey of Faith
Daughter Of The King: Embracing Your Identity In Christ
Determination and Dedication Building Strong Faith As A Young Man
Walking Through Walls God's Power to Part the Storms of Life
David's Song Of Deliverance Praising God Through Every Storm
From Weakness to Warrior: Gideon's Transformation
Why Did Jesus Weep?
Living For God The Call To Be A Living Sacrifice
My Mind Is In A Fog What Do I Do?
Turning The Page Written By Grace
The Calling and Greatness of John the Baptist
For Such a Time Esther's Courageous Stand
From Brokenness To Beauty Written By The Pen of Grace
The Ultimate Guide to Massive Action- From Plans to Reality
A Heart Of Conviction
Serving In The Shadows
Repentance Revealed The Road Back To God
The Chief Sinner Meets The Chief Saviour Reflections On I Timothy 1:15

Answer The Call - 31 Days of Biblical Action
The Birthmark of the Believer
Reflections on Calvary's Cross
The Kingdom Builder Paul's Bold Proclamation of Christ
The Animal Of Pride
The Reach That Restores Christ Love For The Broken
Paul- The Many Roles of a Servant of Christ
Unshakeable Faith- 31 Days of Peace in God's Word
O Come, Let Us Adore Him- A Christmas Devotional
The Shepherd's Voice
The Trail From Vision To Mission
Enabled- Living God's Purpose With Power
Held Back But Not Defeated

Dedication

To you, the reader,

This book is dedicated to your journey—a journey that God Himself has prepared for you. Just as He enabled Paul to carry out a divine calling against impossible odds, so He has also enabled you. You may feel the weight of challenges, moments of doubt, or even seasons of feeling unprepared for the path ahead. Yet, as you hold this book, remember that you, too, have been enabled by the One who calls, equips, and sustains. The same God who strengthened Paul to stand firm, endure trials, and bring hope to countless lives, has empowered you with that same divine strength, wisdom, and courage.

In every page of this book, may you find reminders of His faithfulness—a faithfulness that goes before you, walks beside you, and surrounds you. God's purpose for your life is not a distant dream or a lofty ideal; it is as real and present as the breath in your lungs. Just as Paul was empowered to share the message of hope and love with the world, you, too, are given strength, purpose, and a unique calling to live out in your own time, place, and way. God's enabling power knows no limits, no boundaries, and no exclusions. His power works through your weaknesses, builds upon your strengths, and shines through every part of who you are.

The journey you are about to embark on is one of discovery—of understanding how deeply God loves you, how purposefully He created you, and how tirelessly He equips you each day to fulfill His calling. You don't walk alone; you walk with the One who empowers every step, every word, and every act of faith. His Spirit is your guide, and His presence is your strength, reminding you that just as Paul was enabled, you, too, have been given everything you need to live out God's purpose with courage and confidence.

As you read each daily message, may your heart be encouraged and your spirit strengthened. May you see that God has not asked you to rely on your own strength but on His limitless power—a power that transforms, sustains, and brings life to all that He touches. You are equipped by the One who sees you fully, who loves you completely, and who has a plan for you that is beyond your imagination.

This book is dedicated to you and to the God who has already enabled you for the journey ahead. May you grow in faith, find strength in His promises, and live each day with the assurance that His power is at work within you, guiding you to fulfill a purpose only you can accomplish. You are not alone; you are empowered, sustained, and deeply loved. May this be a journey that reminds you of who you are in Christ and of the unstoppable strength you carry as one whom God has enabled.

"And I thank Christ Jesus our Lord, who hath enabled me." — I Timothy 1:12

To every heart seeking strength, to every spirit longing for purpose—this journey is for you.

"Enabled: Living God's Purpose With Power" is a 31-day guide through Scripture's unshakeable truth: we are not alone in our walk with God. Just as He enabled Paul, He also equips us to overcome fears, face trials, and live with unwavering courage. Each day brings a fresh revelation, inviting us to exchange our weakness for His strength, our doubt for His purpose. Through daily reflections, practical insights, and guided prayers, may you come to know the enabling power of God that sustains and empowers you every step of the way.

This devotional is more than words on a page; it's a call to live confidently in God's presence, knowing His power is actively at work within you.

Introduction
Chapter 1 – Empowered
Chapter 3 – Enlightened
Chapter 4 – Equipped
Chapter 5 – Edified
Chapter 6 – Established
Chapter 7 – Endowed
Chapter 8 – Entrusted
Chapter 9 – Enriched
Chapter 10 - Enduring
Chapter 11 – Energized
Chapter 12 – Elevated
Chapter 13 – Exalted
Chapter 14 – Emboldened
Chapter 15 - Enabled to Evangelize
Chapter 16 – Embraced
Chapter 17 – Exemplary
Chapter 18 – Engaged
Chapter 19 - Enabled for Endurance
Chapter 20 – Empathetic
Chapter 21 – Exhorted
Chapter 22 – Enlisted
Chapter 23 – Entrenched
Chapter 24 - Encompassed by Grace
Chapter 25 - Enabled for Eternity
Chapter 26 - Encircled by Protection
Chapter 27 - Empowered for Excellence
Chapter 28 – Enlarged
Chapter 29 - Endued with Power
Chapter 30 - Entrusted with Influence
Chapter 31 - Enabled to Encourage
Conclusion

Introduction

The 31-day devotional book "Enabled: Living God's Purpose With Power" is designed to help believers discover the strength and purpose God has for each of us, taking us through a journey to deepen our walk with the Lord. Every day in this devotional brings readers face-to-face with a powerful truth from Scripture, rooted in the timeless wisdom of the King James Version, and each message focuses on God's enabling power—how He equips us, sustains us, and strengthens us to live out His calling. Based on the principle in I Timothy 1:12, where Paul says, "And I thank Christ Jesus our Lord, who hath enabled me," this devotional reminds us that just as God enabled Paul to face enormous trials, He enables us to live with confidence, purpose, and resilience in today's world. Life is often filled with challenges, doubts, and fears that can weigh us down or make us feel insufficient, but this devotional speaks directly to those feelings, encouraging readers to exchange their weaknesses for God's strength. Each daily entry includes Scripture reflections, practical insights, and guided prayers, inviting readers to grow closer to God by recognizing that we are never called to live the Christian life alone or in our own strength. Instead, "Enabled: Living God's Purpose With Power" shows us how God's power is actively available to us, working through us to accomplish His will.

As you journey through each day's message, you'll be reminded of how God empowers us to overcome fear, endure trials, serve others, and live with courage even when the path is difficult. By the end of the 31 days, readers will have a clearer understanding of how to rely on God's strength rather than their own, finding that even in the most challenging moments, His grace is sufficient, His love is constant, and His purpose for us is unshakable. Each devotion centers on a characteristic of God's enabling power, such as courage, peace, endurance, wisdom, and faithfulness, allowing readers to see how God's presence strengthens us in every aspect of life. This devotional is ideal for anyone who feels overwhelmed, uncertain, or simply wants to grow stronger in faith. As you read, you'll discover that God's enabling power is not only for those we read about in Scripture, like Paul, but it's for every believer today. This book becomes a guide, reminding us to keep our eyes on Christ, to trust His timing, and to walk confidently in His purpose. Whether you are new to faith or have been walking with the Lord for years, "Enabled: Living God's Purpose With Power" provides a month of uplifting, insightful, and grounding devotionals that will help transform your relationship with God, giving you the tools to live each day empowered, encouraged, and equipped to fulfill His calling in your life.

Chapter 1 – Empowered

In life, we often feel the weight of our own limitations—our struggles, fears, and weaknesses—and sometimes it seems impossible to do what we feel called to do. But God gives us a powerful promise: we are empowered and enabled by His Spirit, not by our own might or power. In Zechariah 4:6, God's message is clear: "Not by might, nor by power, but by my spirit, saith the LORD of hosts." This means that the strength and ability we need to fulfill His calling don't come from within ourselves; they come from God's Spirit working through us. No matter how limited we may feel, God's Spirit is limitless, and He gives us the empowerment we need to serve Him, overcome challenges, and live out the purpose He has for us. Being empowered by God's Spirit means we don't have to rely on our own understanding or our own abilities, which can be flawed and weak. Instead, we can trust that God's Spirit will guide us, giving us wisdom, courage, and strength beyond what we could ever have on our own. This empowerment is available to every believer who calls on God and asks for His help. God's Spirit fills us with peace in moments of fear, with strength when we feel weak, and with direction when we feel lost. Just as God enabled prophets, apostles, and believers throughout Scripture, He enables us today to do things we never thought possible. When we feel inadequate, God's Spirit reminds us that His power is greater than any obstacle. Through this empowerment, we can live with confidence, knowing that it is God who equips us and that we are not alone in our journey. As believers, we are vessels for God's Spirit, and He works in us and through us to accomplish His will. Each time we face a challenge, whether it's in relationships, work, or even in our own faith journey, we can remember that we are not relying on human strength but on divine strength. This is the beauty of being empowered by God's Spirit—it transforms our weaknesses into opportunities for God's glory to shine. When we surrender to His Spirit, we allow God to work through us, accomplishing far more than we ever could alone. This empowerment is also a source of encouragement, reminding us that no task is too great when God's Spirit is with us. It lifts the burden of feeling like we have to do everything ourselves and shifts our perspective to rely on God's limitless power. We are reminded that God's Spirit has been given to us as a helper, a comforter, and a guide, walking with us through every situation. In moments when life feels overwhelming, we can draw strength from this truth, knowing that we have been chosen and equipped by God Himself. Just as God empowered the disciples, even when they faced persecution and hardship, He empowers us today to face our challenges with courage and resilience. The Spirit not only strengthens us but also fills us with hope, giving us the endurance to press on even when the journey seems tough. Being empowered by God's Spirit means living with the assurance that His presence is within us, equipping us to overcome, to serve, and to fulfill His purpose for our lives. This empowerment is not temporary; it is a continuous source of strength and encouragement. As long as we stay close to God, seeking His Spirit daily, we will find that we are empowered to handle whatever comes our way, to live out the calling He has placed on our lives, and to bring glory to His name in everything we do. This empowerment is the foundation of our faith, a constant reminder that we are not alone, and that God's Spirit enables us to live a life full of purpose, love, and impact.

Chapter 2 – Encouraged

In life, we all face difficult times, moments when we feel overwhelmed, discouraged, or even afraid. But as Christians, we have a powerful promise from God that brings us encouragement and strength in those dark moments. Joshua 1:9 reminds us, "Be strong and of a good courage; be not afraid, neither be thou dismayed: for the LORD thy God is with thee whithersoever thou goest." This verse isn't just words on a page; it's a declaration of God's unchanging presence and support, a reminder that we don't walk through our struggles alone. God calls us to be strong and courageous, not because we have all the answers or the strength on our own, but because He is with us every step of the way. He promises to lift us up and encourage us, giving us what we need to keep going even when the journey feels impossible. God's encouragement is a divine strength that fills our hearts, helps us stand firm, and enables us to face challenges without fear. Just as He was with Joshua, leading him through unknown territory and daunting tasks, God is with us in whatever challenges we face. His presence brings peace to our troubled hearts, reassurance to our minds, and courage to our spirits, reminding us that no situation is too big for Him to handle. When we feel discouraged, we can turn to Him in prayer, and He will renew our strength, lifting the weight of our burdens. God's encouragement doesn't mean we won't face hard times; rather, it means He will give us the strength to endure them, teaching us to lean on Him and grow through every trial. He becomes our source of hope, lifting us up when we're weary, reminding us of His love, and helping us to keep pressing on. The Bible is full of stories of people who were encouraged by God in their toughest moments—David, facing Goliath; Elijah, feeling alone and exhausted; Paul, facing persecution. In each of these moments, God didn't remove the challenge, but He encouraged and strengthened His people to overcome it, showing them that His power was enough. For us today, this same encouragement is available. Every time we feel like we're not strong enough, God's words remind us that His strength is made perfect in our weakness. He tells us not to be afraid or dismayed because His presence is constant and His power is limitless. His encouragement is more than just a pat on the back; it's a lifeline, a real and tangible source of strength that we can rely on. When we trust in God's promise, we find the courage to keep moving forward, even in the face of fear or uncertainty. His encouragement transforms our perspective, helping us to see that challenges are opportunities to grow, to trust Him more deeply, and to see His power at work in our lives. When life gets hard, and we feel like giving up, God is there to lift us up, to speak words of encouragement to our hearts, and to remind us of His faithfulness. He gives us peace in the storm, joy in sorrow, and hope in despair. Being encouraged by God means knowing that we don't have to face life's difficulties alone or in our own strength. Instead, we can rest in the knowledge that the God who created the universe, the One who conquered death, is on our side, lifting us up and cheering us on. We can face each day with courage because we are not alone; God is with us, and He is for us. His encouragement is like a shield that guards our hearts and minds, helping us to rise above fear and walk in faith. So, whenever we feel weak, uncertain, or afraid, let us remember Joshua 1:9 and take heart. Let us be strong and courageous, for the Lord our God is with us wherever we go. His encouragement will carry us through, lifting us up, filling us with strength, and leading us to victory, no matter what challenges we face.

Chapter 3 – Enlightened

In this life, we often find ourselves seeking guidance, understanding, and direction, especially when faced with questions or situations that feel confusing or overwhelming. But as Christians, we are blessed with a source of true enlightenment—God's Word. In Psalm 119:130, we are reminded, "The entrance of thy words giveth light; it giveth understanding unto the simple." This verse teaches us that through the Word of God, we are given light for our path, wisdom to navigate life's challenges, and spiritual insight that we cannot gain on our own. God's Word has the power to open our eyes, to show us things as they truly are, and to reveal the truth that we might otherwise miss. It is through His Word that we come to understand His ways, His character, and His will for our lives. When we feel lost or uncertain, His Word becomes a lamp to our feet and a light to our path, showing us the next steps we need to take. Being enlightened by God's Word means that we don't have to rely on our own limited understanding. Instead, we can look to His wisdom, which is perfect, pure, and always trustworthy. The Bible provides us with answers to life's biggest questions—about who God is, who we are, and what our purpose is. This enlightenment brings us peace because we know that the wisdom we receive is not from ourselves but from the One who created all things and knows the beginning from the end.

As we read and meditate on Scripture, God reveals His truths to us in ways that transform our minds and hearts. He helps us see things from His perspective, which is higher and wiser than our own. This spiritual insight allows us to make decisions that honor Him, to avoid pitfalls, and to live lives that reflect His love and grace. Even the "simple," those without worldly wisdom or experience, can understand God's truth when they seek Him through His Word. This is because God's Word is not complicated or out of reach—it is accessible to all who humbly seek it. The Holy Spirit also plays a vital role in enlightening us, helping us understand the depths of Scripture and applying it to our lives. He opens our eyes to the meaning of God's Word and how it relates to our daily situations, teaching us how to live in a way that brings glory to God.

Through this enlightenment, we are equipped to face challenges with confidence and wisdom, knowing that God's Word provides the answers we need. It protects us from being deceived by the world's lies and gives us the clarity to discern right from wrong. In times of confusion, God's Word offers us certainty. In moments of doubt, it gives us faith. And in times of darkness, it brings us light. The Bible is like a treasure chest filled with gems of wisdom, waiting for us to open and discover all that God wants to teach us. This enlightenment isn't just for our own benefit; it enables us to help others, to share God's truth with love, and to be a light in a dark world. When we are filled with the wisdom of God's Word, we can encourage, guide, and uplift those around us, pointing them to the truth that brings life and freedom.

Being enlightened by God's Word also deepens our relationship with Him, as we come to know His heart and His promises more fully. It builds our faith, strengthens our hope, and empowers us to live out His will. Every day, as we study and apply His Word, we grow in wisdom and understanding, becoming more like Christ and more able to fulfill the calling He has for each of us. The Bible is not just a book of rules or history; it is the living Word of God, powerful and transformative. As we allow its truths to fill our minds, we are changed from the inside out, gaining a peace and clarity that only God can give. We are reminded that God's wisdom is always available to us, that He is eager to reveal His truth to those who seek it. So let us turn to His Word with open hearts and minds, ready to be enlightened, strengthened, and guided by the One who loves us and knows what is best for us.

Chapter 4 – Equipped

In our journey as Christians, one of the most encouraging truths we can hold onto is that we are equipped by God with everything we need to serve Him and fulfill His purpose for our lives. In 2 Timothy 3:17, it says, "That the man of God may be perfect, thoroughly furnished unto all good works." This verse is a powerful reminder that God doesn't leave us unprepared for the tasks He calls us to do. Instead, He provides us with all the spiritual tools necessary to carry out good works, to love and serve others, and to spread the Gospel effectively. When we become followers of Christ, God equips us with the Holy Spirit, who empowers us, guides us, and helps us understand His Word. The Holy Spirit is our greatest tool, filling us with the strength and wisdom we need to face life's challenges and to serve others with grace and compassion. God has given each believer unique gifts and abilities, such as teaching, encouragement, leadership, and service, which are meant to be used for His glory and the benefit of others. We may not always see these gifts within ourselves, but when we step out in faith and begin to serve, we discover the talents and skills God has placed within us.

Being equipped also means having access to God's Word, which is a powerful resource for instruction and inspiration. The Bible is filled with teachings, stories, and guidance that equip us to handle various situations in life. When we study the Scriptures, we learn how to respond to trials, how to encourage others, and how to live in a way that honors God. God's Word prepares us not just intellectually but also spiritually, so we can discern right from wrong, make wise decisions, and share His love effectively with those around us. Every time we read and meditate on the Bible, we are being thoroughly furnished for every good work that lies ahead. God's tools are not just for our personal benefit; they are also meant to equip us to be a blessing to others. When we embrace our calling to serve, we find that we are part of something much bigger than ourselves. We are joining God in His mission to bring hope, healing, and love to a world that desperately needs it.

Moreover, being equipped by God encourages us to be confident in our abilities, knowing that we do not rely on our strength alone. God promises to work through us, to use our weaknesses to showcase His power, and to turn our inadequacies into opportunities for His glory. This means that when we feel overwhelmed or unsure of ourselves, we can remember that it is not about our ability but about God's capability to work through us. He has chosen us to be His hands and feet, and He will provide everything necessary to fulfill His mission. As we step out in faith and serve, we will discover the depths of God's provision, whether that is through the support of other believers, unexpected resources, or the wisdom we receive in prayer. God equips us not just for the tasks we are familiar with, but also for the challenges we cannot anticipate. This empowerment gives us the courage to try new things, to step out of our comfort zones, and to engage with our communities in ways we might never have thought possible.

The assurance of being equipped means we can face any situation with confidence, knowing that God has prepared us for whatever lies ahead. We are reminded that our preparation does not end with our initial calling; it is a continual process. God keeps equipping us throughout our lives as we grow in faith and as we encounter new challenges. He teaches us through experiences, trials, and the relationships we build with others. Each moment spent in service adds to our spiritual toolbox, helping us to become more skilled and effective in sharing His love. This ongoing equipping process encourages us to keep learning, growing, and relying on God's grace. As we engage in the work of the Lord, we realize that we are part of a community of believers, all equipped and working together for the same purpose. The synergy of our gifts and talents creates a powerful impact that can transform lives and spread God's love throughout the world.

In every act of service, no matter how small, we reflect the love of Christ and fulfill our role as His disciples. Whether we are helping a neighbor, volunteering in a church, or simply sharing a kind word, we are living out the purpose for which we have been equipped. This encourages us to remain faithful, knowing that every contribution matters in God's plan. Our lives become a testimony of God's equipping power, showing others that they too can be empowered and equipped to serve. So let us embrace the truth that we are equipped by God for every good work, confidently stepping into the roles He has called us to fulfill, fully trusting that He will provide us with everything we need to succeed. In doing so, we honor Him and inspire others to seek their own calling, knowing that through Christ, they too can be thoroughly furnished to accomplish great things for His Kingdom.

Chapter 5 – Edified

Being edified means being built up in our faith, strengthened, and encouraged by God's Word and His presence in our lives. In Ephesians 4:12, we learn that God's desire is for "the perfecting of the saints, for the work of the ministry, for the edifying of the body of Christ." This verse teaches us that God wants us to grow in faith, to be built up so that we are strong in Him, and to be equipped to do His work in the world. To be edified is to be like a building that is constructed carefully, with a solid foundation, growing piece by piece into something strong and beautiful. In our Christian walk, this building up happens as we spend time in God's Word, learning His truths and letting them take root in our hearts. The Bible is filled with teachings that correct us, inspire us, and guide us, helping us to become more like Christ. Each time we read the Scriptures, we are being built up in wisdom, patience, kindness, and love. God's Word shapes us and gives us strength to face life's challenges, teaching us how to walk in righteousness and to be a light to others. The process of edification also involves God's presence, as His Spirit works in our hearts, comforting us, guiding us, and drawing us closer to Him.

When we are edified, we are not easily shaken by the troubles of life, because we have a firm foundation in God's promises. His Word and presence provide stability, so that even in storms, we are anchored and secure. The more we are built up in faith, the more we find ourselves able to stand firm, resist temptation, and make wise choices. Edification strengthens our relationship with God, making us more confident in His love and more aware of His power working in us. This building up isn't just for our benefit; it prepares us to serve others, to be a source of encouragement and strength to those around us. As we grow in faith, we become part of the "body of Christ," contributing to the growth of the entire church. Each believer plays a role, and when we are built up, we can help to build up others, whether through a kind word, a helping hand, or by sharing the Gospel. Being edified by God also brings joy and fulfillment, as we see His purposes unfold in our lives.

The more we are built up, the more we recognize our value and purpose in God's kingdom, knowing that He has a unique plan for each of us. This encouragement allows us to move forward with courage and enthusiasm, ready to face challenges because we know we are not alone. God is constantly with us, building us up, piece by piece, strengthening our character and faith. In times of difficulty, we find ourselves turning to His Word for reassurance, and each time we do, our faith grows stronger. Edification isn't an instant process; it is gradual, requiring patience and a willing heart. But as we commit to spending time in God's presence, seeking Him in prayer, and studying His Word, we see the transformation over time. Our thoughts become more aligned with His, our hearts more open to His guidance, and our lives more reflective of His love.

This building up in faith not only blesses us but also those around us. When others see our peace, joy, and resilience, they are encouraged to seek the same relationship with God. We become a living testimony of His goodness, showing others that faith in Christ brings strength, purpose, and hope. To be edified is to be filled with God's truth and presence, to become more than we could ever be on our own. It's God's way of preparing us for His work, molding us into people who can withstand trials and who can spread His love to a world in need. Edification is a lifelong journey, one that deepens our relationship with God and makes us more like Christ. We are continually being built up, not by our own efforts, but by God's grace and power. This journey is one of joy, growth, and discovery, as we learn more about God's character and His plans for us.

As we let God build us up, we find peace that surpasses understanding and a joy that endures through all circumstances. We learn to rely on Him fully, trusting that He will continue the good work He has begun in us. Each day, we can choose to be edified by seeking His presence, reading His Word, and allowing His Spirit to guide us. As we do, we are strengthened for whatever lies ahead, equipped to serve, and blessed to be a blessing to others.

Chapter 6 – Established

Being established in our faith means being made firm in purpose and grounded in the truth of God's Word. It's about having a solid foundation that keeps us steady, no matter what challenges or storms come our way. In 1 Peter 5:10, we are reminded that "the God of all grace... make you perfect, stablish, strengthen, settle you." This verse encourages us with the promise that God Himself, out of His grace, is the one who establishes us. He is the one who makes us firm, strengthens us, and gives us the stability we need to stand strong in our faith. Life is full of trials, temptations, and confusing situations that can shake us, but when we are established in God's truth, we are able to stay strong, with our feet planted on His promises. Being established doesn't mean we won't face hard times; it means that in those times, we won't be uprooted because we are deeply rooted in God's Word.

To be established is to have a purpose that doesn't waver, a faith that doesn't crumble under pressure. It means that we know who we are in Christ and what He has called us to do. God's truth becomes the solid rock on which we stand, giving us confidence and direction in all areas of life. When we are established in Him, we are not easily swayed by the opinions of others or by the ever-changing values of the world. We know where we stand, and we know why we stand there. God's Word becomes our compass, guiding our thoughts, actions, and decisions. The more we learn His truth, the more grounded we become, able to discern what is right and to resist what is wrong. This grounding helps us to live with integrity, making choices that reflect God's will and not the pressures around us.

Being established by God means that our lives are marked by stability and peace. Even when we face situations that are difficult or confusing, we can rest in the knowledge that God is with us, giving us the strength to persevere. His truth brings clarity in moments of doubt and courage in times of fear. Just as a tree with deep roots can withstand strong winds, so too can we withstand life's challenges when we are rooted in God's promises. To be established also means that we are growing, continually learning and deepening in our relationship with God. He is not finished with us; rather, He is constantly shaping us, teaching us, and building us up so that we become more and more like Christ.

This process of being established is not something we achieve on our own. It is God's work in us, and it requires our willingness to surrender to Him, to seek Him, and to trust His timing. He uses every experience—both the joyful moments and the struggles—to strengthen us and to build our character. Through each trial, He is making us more stable, more certain of His love, and more grounded in our faith. As we allow God to establish us, we find that our purpose becomes clearer. We begin to understand the unique role He has for each of us in His kingdom, and we gain the courage to step out and fulfill that purpose. Our confidence is no longer in our abilities but in the One who has called us and who equips us for every good work.

Being established in Christ gives us a sense of security that is not dependent on circumstances. When we know that God is the foundation of our lives, we are able to face challenges without fear, trusting that He will guide us and hold us steady. This stability allows us to be a source of strength and encouragement to others as well. When people see the peace and firmness in our lives, they are drawn to the stability that comes from a relationship with God. We become living examples of His faithfulness, showing others that a life built on His truth is unshakable.

In every season of life, God is there, working to establish us, to make us firm, and to deepen our roots in His love. The world around us may change, and situations may arise that seem to shake everything we know, but God remains constant, a solid foundation that we can depend on. As we stay close to Him, He continues to establish us, giving us the strength to remain true to His calling, to grow in wisdom, and to walk in His purpose with confidence. Being established in God means that our lives are not blown here and there by every wind; rather, we are anchored, with a purpose that is strong and sure.

Chapter 7 – Endowed

Being endowed by God means we are blessed with spiritual gifts, uniquely given to each one of us by the Holy Spirit to serve others and bring glory to God. In 1 Corinthians 12:7, we learn, "But the manifestation of the Spirit is given to every man to profit withal." This verse is a beautiful reminder that every believer has been gifted by the Spirit, not just for their own benefit, but for the good of all. These gifts are not earned; they are graciously given to us by God, who knows exactly what each of us needs to fulfill our unique role in His kingdom. To be endowed by God means that He has equipped us in special ways to make a difference in the lives of others, to support, to encourage, and to build up His people. These spiritual gifts come in many forms—some are given the gift of teaching, others the gift of encouragement, some the gift of faith, and others the gift of wisdom, healing, or service. Every gift, no matter how small it may seem, has a significant purpose. Together, these gifts create a rich and vibrant body of believers, each member contributing in their unique way to fulfill God's purpose on earth.

When we recognize that we are endowed with these spiritual gifts, we realize that we have a responsibility to use them faithfully. God didn't give us these gifts to keep to ourselves, but to share with others, to strengthen the church, and to show His love to the world. When we use our gifts, we are joining in God's mission, allowing His Spirit to work through us to touch lives and make a lasting impact. This endowment is a reminder that we are not powerless; rather, we are equipped with God's strength, and we are capable of making a difference. Spiritual gifts are not about status or recognition, but about serving with humility and love, using what God has given us to bring light, healing, and encouragement to those around us. In a world that often values material success and personal achievement, God's endowment calls us to a higher purpose—serving others selflessly, pointing them to Christ, and glorifying Him through our actions.

When we embrace our spiritual gifts, we discover a deeper sense of purpose, understanding that we each play a vital role in God's plan. Even when we feel ordinary or unqualified, God's endowment reminds us that He has chosen us, equipped us, and called us to be His hands and feet. Our gifts, combined with the gifts of others, create a powerful force for good, as each member of the body of Christ contributes to the whole. Just as each part of the physical body has a unique function, so do each of us in the body of Christ. Some are called to preach, others to teach, some to encourage, and others to show mercy. No gift is too small, and no role is insignificant in God's kingdom. The beauty of being endowed by God is that we are given exactly what we need to fulfill our role, and together, as we each play our part, the body of Christ is made complete and effective.

This endowment also teaches us to value and appreciate the gifts of others, recognizing that we need one another. No one person possesses every gift, and that's by God's perfect design. He has created us to depend on each other, to work together, and to grow as a community of faith. When we see someone using their gift to bless others, it should inspire us to do the same. Instead of comparing ourselves to others, we can rejoice in the diversity of gifts within the church, knowing that together, we are stronger and more effective. Each of us has something unique to offer, and when we all use our gifts in unity, we reflect the fullness of God's love and grace.

Being endowed with spiritual gifts is not only a blessing, but a calling to action. It means we are equipped to face the challenges that come with serving others, and we are empowered by God's Spirit to bring His love into every situation. Whether we are comforting the hurting, encouraging the weary, teaching the truth, or simply showing kindness, our gifts are tools that God uses to work through us. Even when we feel inadequate, we can trust that God's Spirit is working in us, helping us to accomplish what we could never do on our own. This reliance on His Spirit is what makes our gifts powerful, for it is not our own strength but God's strength that brings true change. As we surrender our lives to Him and use our gifts for His glory, we experience the joy of partnering with God in His work, and we see the amazing ways He can use us to bless others.

Being endowed by God with spiritual gifts reminds us that we are a part of something bigger than ourselves. It's about being a part of God's family, working together to fulfill His mission, and making a lasting difference in the lives of those around us. When we are faithful in using our gifts, we are fulfilling our purpose, and we are drawing closer to God as we see Him working through us. Every time we use our gifts, we are reminded of His love, His wisdom, and His grace. We are reminded that He sees value in each of us, that He has a plan for each of us, and that He is with us every step of the way. Our gifts are a testament to His goodness, a reminder that He has not left us alone, but has given us everything we need to live out our faith.

So let us embrace our endowment, recognizing that these gifts are sacred, given to us by God to build His kingdom and to bring hope and healing to a world in need. Let us be faithful stewards of what He has entrusted to us, using our gifts with gratitude, humility, and joy. And as we do, we will find that not only are we blessing others, but we ourselves are blessed, experiencing the deep fulfillment that comes from living out God's purpose.

Chapter 8 – Entrusted

To be entrusted with the Gospel is a profound responsibility and an incredible privilege. In 1 Thessalonians 2:4, Paul says, "But as we were allowed of God to be put in trust with the gospel, even so we speak." This verse reminds us that God has chosen us, not because of our own merit, but by His grace, to carry the message of hope, love, and salvation to a world in need. Being entrusted with the Gospel means that God sees us as worthy stewards of His truth, calling us to share it with sincerity, faithfulness, and dedication. The Gospel is not just a story or a set of beliefs—it is the living message of Christ's sacrifice, the promise of redemption, and the invitation to eternal life. When we truly understand what it means to be entrusted with such a gift, we recognize that sharing it is not optional; it is a sacred duty that has been given to us by the Creator Himself.

God could have chosen any method to spread His message, but He chose to work through people, through us, so that we might bring His light to others. This calling is not reserved for a select few; it is for every believer, from the youngest to the oldest, to take the Gospel and make it known. Whether we are speaking to a large crowd or simply sharing our faith with a friend, we are fulfilling the trust that God has placed in us. When we are entrusted with the Gospel, we are called to live in a way that reflects the love and truth of Christ, showing others by our actions and words that the Gospel is real and powerful. Each day, we have opportunities to make a difference in the lives of those around us, to plant seeds of faith, to encourage the weary, and to give hope to the hopeless. God has given us this responsibility, and with it comes the assurance that His Spirit is with us, guiding us, and giving us the courage to speak boldly and lovingly.

Being entrusted with the Gospel means we must handle it with care, knowing that it is precious and life-changing. This responsibility is not something to be taken lightly or treated casually. God has placed His trust in us, asking us to be ambassadors of His love, to carry His truth to those who are lost, and to do so faithfully. It is a call to be faithful, to speak the truth even when it is difficult, and to stand firm in the face of opposition. The world may challenge our beliefs, question our motives, or even reject the message we share, but we are not called to change the message to make it more acceptable; we are called to speak the truth as it is, trusting that God will work in the hearts of those who hear it. Our job is to be faithful to the Gospel, to share it with love and humility, leaving the results in God's hands.

When we are entrusted with the Gospel, we are also given the privilege of seeing lives transformed by its power. There is nothing more fulfilling than witnessing someone come to know Christ, to see the joy and freedom that comes from accepting His love and grace. Each time we share the Gospel, we are sowing seeds that can grow into a harvest of faith, drawing people closer to God and helping them find peace, purpose, and salvation. This responsibility brings both joy and urgency, reminding us that our time on earth is limited, and that every moment counts. We do not know who God will place in our path or how He will use our words to reach others, but we know that He has a plan, and He has chosen us to be a part of it. Every encounter, every conversation, and every opportunity to share our faith is a chance to fulfill the trust that God has given us.

Being entrusted with the Gospel also means living a life that honors God and reflects His love to others. It is not enough to speak the truth; we must also live it, showing by our actions that we believe what we preach. Our lives should be a testimony to the power of the Gospel, a living example of the hope and transformation that comes from knowing Christ. When people see our kindness, patience, and integrity, they should be drawn to the source of our faith, wanting to know the God who has changed us. This is why it is so important to walk in integrity, to be mindful of our words and actions, and to remember that we represent Christ in everything we do. Being entrusted with the Gospel is a call to live a life that is consistent with our faith, to be a light in a world that desperately needs hope, and to be an example of God's love to all we encounter.

As we carry out this responsibility, we are reminded that we do not do it alone. God has given us His Spirit to empower us, His Word to guide us, and a community of believers to support us. When we feel discouraged, unsure, or inadequate, we can turn to God for strength, knowing that He will equip us for the task He has given us. He does not expect us to be perfect; He simply asks us to be faithful, to trust Him, and to rely on His strength. Being entrusted with the Gospel is a journey of growth, as we learn to depend more fully on God, to step out in faith, and to see His hand at work in ways we never could have imagined. It is a journey filled with challenges, but also with blessings, as we see God's faithfulness and grace in every step we take.

Let us remember that being entrusted with the Gospel is a high calling, a sacred responsibility, and a beautiful privilege. It is an honor to share the message of Christ's love, to bring light to darkness, and to offer hope to those in despair. May we embrace this calling with joy, knowing that we are fulfilling God's purpose for our lives, and may we be faithful in every opportunity He gives us to share His truth. In doing so, we will not only honor the trust that God has placed in us, but we will also find the deep joy and fulfillment that comes from serving Him and making a difference in the lives of others.

Chapter 9 – Enriched

Being enriched spiritually means that we are blessed and filled with the wisdom and grace of God, a gift that brings depth and purpose to every aspect of our lives. Colossians 2:2-3 tells us about this incredible blessing, saying, "In whom are hid all the treasures of wisdom and knowledge." This verse reminds us that in Jesus Christ, we find all the wisdom and knowledge we could ever need, treasures that go beyond what the world can offer. To be spiritually enriched by God is to be filled with His truth, guided by His wisdom, and strengthened by His grace, all of which equip us to live with purpose and joy. God's wisdom is a treasure because it leads us in paths of righteousness, helps us make decisions that honor Him, and gives us insight into His will for our lives. This wisdom is not something we can achieve on our own; it is a divine gift that comes from walking closely with God, studying His Word, and allowing His Spirit to guide us. As we seek God, He enriches our minds and hearts, opening our understanding to see things from His perspective, which is higher and wiser than ours.

God's enrichment in our lives is not only intellectual but also deeply spiritual. It fills us with peace in times of trouble, hope in moments of doubt, and strength when we feel weak. His grace enriches us, reminding us that we are loved unconditionally and that we have been given the gift of salvation through Jesus. This grace transforms us, helping us to forgive others, to love more deeply, and to live with compassion. God's grace is like a wellspring that never runs dry, continually refreshing and renewing us so that we are equipped to face each day with confidence. Spiritual enrichment means that we are not empty or lacking, but rather filled with everything we need to live a life that pleases God. We become like vessels overflowing with His goodness, ready to share that love and wisdom with others.

Being spiritually enriched also means growing in our relationship with God, becoming more attuned to His voice, and more aware of His presence in our lives. As we grow closer to Him, we begin to see the world differently, recognizing His hand in all things and learning to trust Him more fully. His wisdom teaches us how to navigate the challenges of life with grace and integrity, and His truth gives us a solid foundation on which to stand. When we face decisions, temptations, or trials, God's enrichment gives us the discernment to choose what is right, to avoid the paths that lead to harm, and to stay grounded in our faith. We are not easily shaken because we know that our wisdom comes from the One who knows all things, who sees the end from the beginning, and who desires only the best for us.

This enrichment also brings joy and fulfillment that the world cannot give. The treasures of wisdom and knowledge in Christ are far greater than material wealth, fame, or earthly success. They are treasures of the soul that satisfy our deepest longings, giving us a sense of purpose and a reason to hope. We are enriched by the promises of God, which assure us of His love, His faithfulness, and His plan for our lives. Even in the midst of trials, we are spiritually rich because we possess something eternal and unshakeable. The world may chase after temporary pleasures, but as Christians, we are blessed with a joy that endures and a peace that surpasses understanding. This spiritual enrichment fills us with contentment, knowing that we are cared for by our Heavenly Father, who provides all that we need.

As we are enriched by God's wisdom and grace, we also become a source of encouragement and strength to others. Our lives become a testimony of God's goodness, showing others the joy and fulfillment that come from knowing Him. When people see the peace, joy, and strength in our lives, they are drawn to the source of our enrichment—Jesus Christ. We are able to share His love, offer guidance, and be a light to those who are struggling. Spiritual enrichment is not just for our benefit; it enables us to impact the world around us, bringing hope and encouragement to those who are lost, weary, or in need of direction. God's wisdom flows through us as we minister to others, helping them to see that they, too, can be filled with His grace and truth.

Being enriched by God is a continual process. As we spend time in His Word, pray, and seek His presence, He continues to pour out His wisdom and grace into our lives, helping us to grow in faith and maturity. We never reach a point where we are fully complete; rather, God is always working in us, deepening our understanding, expanding our compassion, and increasing our ability to live in a way that reflects His love. Each day, as we open our hearts to Him, He fills us anew, equipping us to face whatever challenges come our way. Spiritual enrichment keeps us humble, reminding us that all we have and all we are comes from God. It is His work in us, His Spirit guiding us, and His truth sustaining us.

To be spiritually enriched is to walk in a relationship with God that continually fills us, renews us, and strengthens us. We are blessed beyond measure, not because of anything we have done, but because of who God is—a loving, generous Father who desires to bless His children. He enriches us with wisdom to make good choices, with grace to forgive and love others, and with peace that anchors us in times of trouble. As we receive these treasures from God, we find ourselves living a life that is full, purposeful, and grounded in His truth. Spiritual enrichment transforms us, making us more like Christ and enabling us to fulfill His calling with joy and confidence.

In every season of life, whether in times of joy or sorrow, we can be assured that we are spiritually enriched by God, filled with His wisdom, His grace, and His love. This enrichment is a gift that sustains us, empowers us, and gives us the courage to live boldly for Him. Let us embrace this blessing, allowing God's wisdom and grace to shape our lives, to guide our decisions, and to fill us with a joy that overflows to those around us. With hearts enriched by God, we are equipped to face each day with strength, hope, and purpose, knowing that we are held by the One in whom are hidden all the treasures of wisdom and knowledge.

Chapter 10 - Enduring

Enduring through trials and hardships is one of the greatest challenges in life, yet it is also one of the most rewarding aspects of our faith. The Bible tells us in James 1:12, "Blessed is the man that endureth temptation: for when he is tried, he shall receive the crown of life." This verse reminds us that there is a blessing in enduring, a reward that awaits those who hold fast to their faith, even when life becomes difficult. To endure means to withstand, to keep going, and to remain strong, no matter what obstacles come our way. Life brings many challenges—loss, disappointment, fear, illness, and hardship—and in these times, it can be tempting to give up, to doubt, or to lose hope. But God promises that He will give us the strength we need to endure, to stay faithful, and to keep moving forward. Endurance is not something we have to muster up on our own; it is a gift from God, a strength that He provides to us as we rely on Him. When we are weak, He is strong, and when we feel like we cannot go on, He carries us through.

God's promise of endurance is a reminder that He is always with us, even in the darkest moments. He doesn't promise that we won't face trials, but He does promise that He will be with us, giving us the courage and strength to endure. Just as a tree with deep roots can withstand strong winds, we too can endure life's storms when we are rooted in God's Word and His love. Each trial we face has the potential to strengthen our faith, to teach us perseverance, and to draw us closer to God. Endurance is a process of growth, and every challenge we overcome builds our character, making us stronger and more resilient. God uses these hardships to mold us, to deepen our faith, and to show us His faithfulness. When we endure, we learn to trust God more, to rely on His strength rather than our own, and to see His hand at work in ways we might never have noticed before.

Enduring also teaches us patience, helping us to wait on God's timing and to trust that He knows what is best. Sometimes, God allows trials in our lives to refine us, to teach us lessons that we could not learn any other way. In these moments, endurance means holding on to hope, even when we cannot see the outcome, and believing that God is working all things for our good. It is in the waiting, in the persevering, that we come to know God more deeply, experiencing His comfort, His peace, and His grace. Endurance does not mean that we have to be strong on our own; it means that we lean on God, that we trust Him to provide us with the strength we need to keep going. He is our rock, our refuge, and our source of hope. When we feel like giving up, we can turn to Him, and He will renew our strength, helping us to endure with courage and faith.

As we endure, we also become a witness to others, showing them the power of faith in the midst of hardship. Our endurance is a testimony of God's faithfulness, a light that shines in the darkness, pointing others to the hope and peace that can only be found in Him. When people see us enduring with grace and trust, they are encouraged to seek that same strength in their own lives. Enduring trials allows us to be an example of God's love and power, showing the world that He is with us, no matter what we face. Each time we endure, we grow in our ability to trust God, to find joy in His promises, and to hold fast to our faith. We learn that God is enough, that His grace is sufficient, and that His love will carry us through every trial. This knowledge gives us peace, knowing that no matter what happens, God is in control, and He will bring us through.

The promise of the "crown of life" for those who endure is a reminder of the eternal reward that awaits us. God sees every struggle, every tear, and every effort we make to stay faithful, and He promises that our endurance will not be in vain. The trials we face here on earth are temporary, but the reward that God has prepared for us is eternal. This hope gives us the strength to keep going, to endure with joy, knowing that God has something beautiful waiting for us. Each day, as we face life's challenges, we can remember that God is with us, that He is giving us the strength to endure, and that He is preparing us for something far greater than we can imagine. To endure is to hold onto this hope, to believe that God is faithful, and to trust that He will carry us through, no matter what comes our way.

Chapter 11 – Energized

Being energized by God means experiencing a deep refreshment and renewal that comes not from our own strength, but from His limitless power. Life can be exhausting—our daily struggles, responsibilities, and challenges often leave us feeling drained, weary, and empty. But in Isaiah 40:31, we find a promise that brings hope and strength: "But they that wait upon the LORD shall renew their strength." This verse reminds us that when we rely on God, He will give us the energy and vitality we need to keep going. God's power is endless, and when we feel weak or worn out, He invites us to turn to Him, to rest in His presence, and to draw from His strength. To be energized by God is to experience a kind of refreshment that fills us from the inside out, lifting our spirits, renewing our minds, and giving us the courage to face each new day. This divine energy is not something we can manufacture on our own; it is a gift from God that comes when we take time to seek Him, to wait on Him, and to trust Him.

Waiting on God doesn't mean sitting idly; it means actively placing our hope and faith in Him, believing that He will strengthen us as we lean on Him. When we are connected to God, He becomes the source of our energy, pouring His Spirit into our lives and giving us what we need to move forward. This is a strength that goes beyond physical endurance; it's a spiritual strength that empowers us to face life's challenges with resilience and hope. God's energy fills us with a sense of purpose and passion, reminding us that we are not alone, and that He is working in and through us. As we wait on the Lord, we are filled with His peace, His love, and His joy—all of which energize us and give us the stamina to keep going, even when the journey is difficult.

God's energy is like a well that never runs dry. No matter how many times we come to Him for renewal, He is always ready to fill us up again. In a world that often leaves us feeling empty and fatigued, God offers us a refreshment that cannot be found anywhere else. His energy revives our souls, giving us the motivation to pursue our calling, to serve others, and to live with joy and gratitude. When we feel overwhelmed by life's demands, God's power is there to lift us up, to give us a new perspective, and to remind us that He is in control. This divine energy doesn't just help us survive; it enables us to thrive, to live fully, and to embrace each day with a spirit of hope. When we are energized by God, we are able to approach our responsibilities with a renewed sense of enthusiasm and dedication, knowing that we are not working alone, but with His support.

This energy also helps us to be a source of encouragement to others. When people see the strength and joy that come from being connected to God, they are drawn to that same source of renewal. Our lives become a testimony of God's power, showing others that there is a way to find refreshment that goes beyond the temporary fixes the world offers. When we are energized by God, we are able to serve others selflessly, to uplift those who are struggling, and to shine a light in the darkness. This energy is contagious, inspiring others to seek God's strength for themselves, and to experience the same refreshment and vitality that He offers. We are reminded that God's power is available to everyone who seeks Him, and that His energy is not just for our benefit, but for the benefit of all those around us.

God's energy also helps us to overcome the obstacles that come our way. When we face challenges, disappointments, or setbacks, His strength helps us to rise above them, to persevere, and to keep moving forward with confidence. This divine energy gives us resilience, helping us to stand firm in our faith, to trust in His promises, and to remain hopeful, even in difficult times. It reminds us that we are never alone, that God is with us every step of the way, and that He is our source of strength in every situation. As we rely on Him, we find that we are able to do things we never thought possible, to endure hardships, and to pursue our goals with courage and determination.

To be energized by God is to live with a sense of peace and assurance, knowing that our strength comes from Him. We don't have to rely on our own limited energy, which can easily be depleted; instead, we can draw from God's limitless power, which is always available to us. This allows us to face each day with confidence, knowing that no matter what challenges come our way, we have the strength to overcome them. God's energy gives us the ability to live fully, to love deeply, and to pursue our calling with passion. It fills us with a sense of purpose, reminding us that we are part of something greater than ourselves, and that we are working for His glory.

As we experience this divine energy, we are reminded of God's faithfulness, His love, and His desire to see us thrive. He wants us to live with joy, to find fulfillment in our work, and to have the stamina to serve Him faithfully. This energy is a reminder that God cares about every aspect of our lives, and that He is committed to supporting us, strengthening us, and helping us to succeed. Each day, as we spend time in prayer, reading His Word, and seeking His presence, we are filled with His energy, renewed in our purpose, and ready to face whatever lies ahead.

In every season of life, God's energy is available to us, refreshing us, uplifting us, and giving us the strength to keep going. It is a gift that reminds us of His love, His grace, and His power, and it allows us to live with a sense of joy and gratitude, even in the midst of challenges. When we are energized by God, we are able to live each day to the fullest, to pursue our dreams, and to serve others with a heart of compassion. We are reminded that we are not alone, that God is with us, and that His power is more than enough to sustain us. Let us embrace this gift of divine energy, allowing God to fill us, renew us, and equip us for the journey ahead. With His strength, we can face any challenge, overcome any obstacle, and live a life that reflects His love and His glory.

Chapter 12 – Elevated

To be elevated as a child of God means to be lifted up, honored, and cherished by our Creator, the King of Kings. In Psalm 3:3, we read, "But thou, O LORD, art a shield for me; my glory, and the lifter up of mine head." This beautiful verse reminds us that God is our protector, our strength, and the one who lifts us up in times of trouble, fear, and doubt. He is the one who honors us, not because of our own deeds, but because of His deep love for us. To be elevated by God is to be given a place of honor and value, to know that we are His children, and that He loves us beyond measure. When we feel low, unworthy, or forgotten, God reaches down, lifts our heads, and reminds us that we are His beloved. He treats us as His own, with a love that is pure, unconditional, and everlasting. This elevation is not based on worldly standards or achievements; it is rooted in the identity we have in Christ. We are no longer defined by our past, our failures, or our weaknesses. In God's eyes, we are precious, forgiven, and deeply loved, lifted to a place of honor as part of His family.

God's elevation is not about pride or earthly status; it is a lifting of our spirits, a raising of our hearts, and an assurance that we are seen, known, and valued. He honors us as His own, calling us to stand tall in His grace and to walk in the confidence of His love. The world may try to bring us down, to make us feel small, inadequate, or unworthy, but God's Word reminds us that we are more than conquerors through Him who loves us. We are not defined by what others think of us or by the struggles we face; we are defined by the God who calls us His children and lifts us up. This divine elevation gives us hope, reminding us that no matter how hard life gets, we are held by the One who has overcome it all. He gives us strength when we are weak, courage when we are afraid, and joy even in times of sorrow. God's elevation is a gift that fills our hearts with peace, knowing that we are not alone and that He is always with us, guiding us, protecting us, and lifting us up.

As children of God, we are elevated to a life filled with purpose, dignity, and worth. We are no longer wandering without direction; instead, we are called to live as His ambassadors, representing His love and grace to the world. God lifts us up not just to bless us, but to empower us to be a blessing to others. He calls us to rise above our struggles, to live with hope, and to share that hope with those around us. Being elevated by God changes the way we see ourselves and the world around us. We are no longer limited by our circumstances, because we serve a God who is greater than anything we could ever face. He gives us the strength to overcome, the wisdom to make wise choices, and the courage to step forward in faith. Each time we feel discouraged or defeated, God lifts us, reminding us that we are His and that we are loved.

This elevation by God is a constant source of encouragement, giving us the strength to press on and the confidence to live boldly for Him. Knowing that we are honored by God helps us to walk in humility and gratitude, understanding that everything we have comes from His hand. We don't have to strive for approval or validation from others because we are already lifted up by the One who matters most. God sees our potential, our heart, and our desire to serve Him, and He elevates us as His beloved children. This truth fills us with peace, knowing that our identity is secure in Him. He is the lifter of our heads, the One who restores our joy, renews our strength, and fills us with His love. When we feel low or insignificant, we can turn to God, and He will lift us up, reminding us of our worth and our place in His kingdom.

God's elevation is a reminder that we are never forgotten, never forsaken, and never alone. He sees us, He loves us, and He calls us His own. He lifts us up from the ashes, turns our mourning into joy, and gives us beauty for our brokenness. This lifting up is an act of grace, a gift that we could never earn but that God freely gives because of His great love for us. He wants us to know that we are cherished, that we are valuable, and that we are His. In times of doubt or despair, we can hold onto the truth that God is our shield, our glory, and the lifter up of our heads. He will carry us through every trial, lifting us up in His arms of love, and reminding us that we are His children, honored and blessed.

Chapter 13 – Exalted

To be exalted by God is a profound blessing, a raising up by His hand for His glory and purpose. In 1 Peter 5:6, we are reminded, "Humble yourselves therefore under the mighty hand of God, that he may exalt you in due time." This verse teaches us that when we walk in humility, recognizing our need for God and trusting in His timing, He will lift us up in ways that honor Him. Exaltation from God is not about human fame, power, or success; rather, it is about being positioned and blessed by Him for His divine purposes. When God exalts us, He does so with a purpose, using our lives as a testimony of His grace, love, and power. In a world that often focuses on self-promotion and seeking validation, God calls us to a different path—a path of humility, obedience, and trust in His perfect timing. When we allow God to work in us and through us, He lifts us up in ways that reflect His glory, not ours. He blesses us so that our lives can shine as examples of His goodness, drawing others to Him through the way we live, love, and serve.

Being exalted by God requires patience, as His timing may not align with our own desires or plans. Yet, His timing is always perfect. He knows when we are ready and when our hearts are aligned with His will. Exaltation from God is not rushed or forced; it is a process that takes place as we grow in faith, as we learn to trust Him fully, and as we surrender our own ambitions for His greater plan. In times when we feel overlooked or unappreciated, God's promise to exalt us encourages us to keep walking faithfully, knowing that He sees every act of obedience and every step of humility. He values the quiet, unseen moments of faithfulness just as much as the grand gestures, and in His time, He will raise us up in ways that bring Him honor.

God's exaltation often comes in ways we don't expect. It may not be about achieving status or recognition but rather about being placed in a position where we can make a difference, influence others, or fulfill a specific purpose

He has designed for us. When God exalts us, He does so with a reason, giving us opportunities to serve, to lead, and to represent Him in all we do. This exaltation is a gift of His favor, showing that He trusts us to carry out His work and to use the blessings He gives us to serve others. We are called to use our elevated position, whatever that may be, to reflect His love, grace, and mercy. Every blessing He gives, every way He lifts us up, is meant to point back to Him, to demonstrate His power and goodness in our lives.

Exaltation by God reminds us that our worth and value come from Him alone. We do not need to seek approval from the world or measure ourselves by its standards. God knows our hearts, our struggles, and our desires, and He promises to lift us up when the time is right. This knowledge gives us peace and confidence, knowing that we are secure in His love and purpose. We can let go of the need to prove ourselves, focusing instead on living for His glory and trusting that He will exalt us in His way and in His time. When we are lifted up by God, it is not for our own praise but for His, so that our lives become a reflection of His grace.

As we humble ourselves before God, seeking to serve rather than to be served, He works in our hearts, molding us into vessels that He can use for His kingdom. True exaltation comes from a place of surrender, where we acknowledge that any success, blessing, or honor we receive is by His hand alone. This humility keeps us grounded, reminding us that apart from Him, we can do nothing. We are simply vessels of His glory, called to live in a way that draws others to Him. The exaltation that comes from God is enduring, filled with purpose, and aligned with His eternal plan. It is a far greater honor than any human recognition could ever offer, for it comes from the Creator Himself.

To be exalted by God is to experience His favor in a way that lifts our spirits, strengthens our faith, and deepens our relationship with Him. His favor is a reminder that we are loved, valued, and seen by Him, even in the quiet and hidden parts of our lives. God does not forget His people; He knows each one by name, and He delights in blessing those who walk in His ways. When He exalts us, He does so to show us His faithfulness, to encourage us, and to use our lives as a testimony to His greatness. Every time we experience His exaltation, it strengthens our commitment to serve Him more deeply, to love others more fully, and to live in a way that brings Him honor.

In moments of doubt or discouragement, we can hold onto the promise of God's exaltation, knowing that He has a perfect plan for each of us. No act of humility, no moment of faithfulness goes unnoticed by Him. Even when the world does not see, God sees, and He will reward in His own time. This assurance allows us to live with patience, to serve with joy, and to wait with hope, knowing that God's exaltation is worth the wait. His favor is a precious gift, a lifting of our spirits and lives that fills us with peace, joy, and purpose. As we wait on Him, we learn to find contentment in His presence, to trust in His timing, and to let go of our own agendas, embracing the calling He has placed on our lives.

Let us embrace the path of humility, knowing that as we submit ourselves to God, He will lift us up in ways that bring Him glory. He is our strength, our shield, and the lifter of our heads. When we focus on serving Him, on living for His honor, He will exalt us in ways that exceed our expectations. His exaltation is a gift, a privilege, and a calling, inviting us to live as His beloved children, blessed by His favor and raised up for His glory.

Chapter 14 – Emboldened

To be emboldened as a child of God means to have the courage and confidence to speak His truth without fear, knowing that He is with us every step of the way. In Acts 4:31, we read, "And they spake the word of God with boldness." This verse is a powerful reminder that, with the Holy Spirit's help, we can overcome fear and share the message of hope, love, and salvation that God has given us. Being emboldened by God is not about relying on our own strength or charisma; it's about trusting in His power and His presence in our lives. God gives us the boldness to stand firm in our faith, to declare His goodness, and to be a light in a world that often prefers darkness. When we feel weak, uncertain, or intimidated, God's Spirit fills us with a courage that is not of ourselves, allowing us to speak and live out His truth without hesitation.

Being emboldened doesn't mean we won't feel nervous or afraid at times. Instead, it means that even when fear tries to hold us back, we choose to step forward, trusting that God will give us the words and the strength we need. The early disciples faced incredible opposition, yet they were able to proclaim the Gospel with boldness because they were empowered by the Holy Spirit. This same Spirit lives within us, giving us the courage to speak truth in love, to stand up for what is right, and to be witnesses of Christ's love in our everyday lives. The world around us may challenge or question our beliefs, but God calls us to be unashamed of the Gospel, to let His light shine through us, and to proclaim His truth with confidence.

When we are emboldened by God, we don't let the opinions or criticisms of others silence us. Instead, we remember that we are ambassadors of Christ, called to share His message with a world that desperately needs it. This boldness is not about being loud or confrontational; it's about having a quiet confidence that comes from knowing who we are in Christ and what He has done for us. God gives us the strength to be gentle yet firm, compassionate yet unwavering, loving yet truthful. Our boldness is rooted in our relationship with God, in our knowledge of His Word, and in our trust that He is with us. Every time we speak His truth, we are fulfilling the mission He has given us, bringing hope to those who are lost and guiding others to His light.

Being emboldened also means being willing to stand alone if necessary, to speak up when it's unpopular, and to hold fast to God's truth even when others do not understand. This courage comes from a deep love for God and a desire to honor Him above all else. We know that He has entrusted us with His message, and we take that responsibility seriously. When we are emboldened by God, we are able to push past our fears, our doubts, and our insecurities, focusing instead on the mission He has given us. We become willing to step out of our comfort zones, to reach out to those who are hurting, and to share the hope we have in Christ. This boldness allows us to be a light in the darkness, to be a source of encouragement, and to be a voice of truth in a world that needs to hear it.

As we walk in this boldness, we discover a deeper level of faith and trust in God. Each time we step out in faith, He meets us there, giving us the words, the wisdom, and the courage we need. Being emboldened by God strengthens our relationship with Him, helping us to rely more fully on His power and less on our own. We learn to depend on His guidance, to trust in His promises, and to know that He is always with us. This boldness is not something we muster up on our own; it is a gift from God, a reflection of His strength working in and through us. It reminds us that we are not alone, that we are empowered by the Almighty, and that He is the one who makes us bold.

In every situation, God gives us the opportunity to be a witness for Him, to share His love and truth with those around us. Being emboldened by God allows us to embrace these moments, to speak with confidence, and to trust that He will use our words for His glory. This courage is not about winning arguments or proving a point; it's about showing others the love of Christ, helping them to see His grace, and guiding them toward a relationship with Him. Our boldness is a testimony to God's faithfulness, a reflection of His love, and a reminder that His message is worth sharing. When we speak boldly for God, we are fulfilling the calling He has placed on our lives, living out our faith in a way that honors Him and impacts others.

As we go through life, there will be times when speaking God's truth requires us to take risks, to face criticism, or to endure rejection. Yet, with God's boldness, we are able to withstand these challenges, knowing that He is our strength and our shield. We are reminded that our purpose is to glorify Him, to make His name known, and to share His love with those who are lost. Each time we choose to speak boldly, we are planting seeds of faith, hope, and truth that can change lives and draw people closer to God. God's boldness enables us to be courageous even in the face of fear, to remain steadfast in our convictions, and to trust that He is working through us.

Let us embrace this gift of boldness, allowing God to use us as His vessels, to be His hands and feet, and to be His voice in a world that needs to hear His truth. With God's boldness, we can face any challenge, overcome any obstacle, and live a life that reflects His love and grace. This boldness is a blessing, a privilege, and a calling, inviting us to step forward in faith, to speak truth without fear, and to be a light for Christ in everything we do.

Chapter 15 - Enabled to Evangelize

To be enabled to evangelize means that God gives us the courage, strength, and purpose to share the Gospel, bringing the message of salvation to others with boldness and love. Matthew 28:19 commands us, "Go ye therefore, and teach all nations." This call to "go" is not just for the apostles of old; it is a charge for every Christian, reminding us that we have a purpose in this world—to spread the Good News of Jesus Christ. Evangelism can be daunting; we may feel unprepared, nervous, or unsure of how others will respond. Yet God does not leave us to do this alone. He enables us with His Spirit, filling us with courage and wisdom, guiding our words and actions as we speak about His love and truth. Being enabled to evangelize means that God equips us, not by our own strength, but by His power working through us. Just as He empowered His disciples to preach, teach, and reach out, He empowers us to do the same, transforming lives through the words we share.

When we are enabled to evangelize, we are filled with a sense of purpose, knowing that we are part of God's great plan to reach the world. Evangelism is not just a task; it's a mission that flows from the love we have received from God. When we experience His grace, mercy, and forgiveness, we naturally want to share that joy with others, helping them find the same peace and salvation we have found. Evangelism isn't about having all the answers; it's about sharing our testimony, our faith, and our story, trusting that God will use our words to touch hearts. Through our willingness to speak, God can work in the lives of those who are lost, guiding them to the hope, healing, and life that only He can give.

God gives us the courage to overcome our fears, the wisdom to share in love, and the strength to persevere, even when we face resistance or rejection. Evangelizing doesn't require perfection; it requires a willing heart. God enables us, despite our weaknesses, to be His messengers, reaching out to people with the compassion and kindness of Christ. He uses our unique gifts, personalities, and experiences to connect with others, to show them that His love is real, and to encourage them to turn toward Him. Every act of sharing the Gospel, whether big or small, is valuable. We may never know the full impact of our words, but God does, and He is faithful to use them in ways we might never expect.

When we are enabled by God to evangelize, we are empowered to speak truth in a world filled with confusion, to bring hope where there is despair, and to shine light in places of darkness. God's Spirit moves in us, giving us boldness to speak even when we feel hesitant. Evangelism is not about being forceful or argumentative; it's about offering the gift of salvation with humility and love, knowing that it is God who changes hearts. Our job is to share; His job is to transform. When we realize that the results are in God's hands, we are freed from fear, focusing instead on the joy of sharing our faith and the privilege of being part of His work. This confidence in God's power enables us to speak without fear, knowing that He is with us and that He will accomplish His purpose through us.

Each time we share the Gospel, we are fulfilling the Great Commission, obeying Jesus' command to "teach all nations." This calling gives us a sense of mission, a reason to reach out, and a desire to see lives changed for eternity. Evangelism is an expression of our love for God and for others, a way to spread His kingdom and to make His name known. Through the courage He gives us, we become His ambassadors, carrying the message of reconciliation, peace, and hope to those who need it most. The world is filled with people who are searching for meaning, purpose, and love, and God has chosen us, His children, to bring His truth to them.

As we step out in faith, God uses us to break down barriers, to build connections, and to plant seeds of faith in the hearts of others. We may not always see immediate results, but God assures us that His Word does not return void. Every time we share the Gospel, we are planting seeds that can grow and bear fruit in ways we might not see. Evangelism is a journey of faith, where we trust that God is working in every conversation, every testimony, and every act of kindness. He is constantly moving, preparing hearts, and using our efforts to bring people closer to Him. This knowledge gives us the courage to keep going, even when it's difficult, to keep speaking, even when it's uncomfortable, and to keep loving, even when it's challenging.

Being enabled to evangelize also deepens our own faith, as we see God's faithfulness and power at work in the lives of others. As we share the Gospel, we are reminded of the beauty of our own salvation, the wonder of His grace, and the joy of His presence. This calling strengthens our relationship with God, helping us to rely on Him, to seek His guidance, and to celebrate His goodness. Each opportunity to evangelize becomes an opportunity to grow closer to Him, to deepen our trust, and to see His love poured out through us. We begin to see people not as strangers, but as individuals whom God loves, who are made in His image, and who are in need of His salvation.

God's enabling power gives us a heart for others, a passion to reach out, and a desire to see His kingdom expand. As we share the Gospel, we are reminded that we are part of something greater than ourselves—a divine mission that stretches across time, reaching souls for Christ, and making an impact that will last for eternity. Evangelism is not a burden but a blessing, a gift that allows us to be part of God's work in the world. Each time we share His truth, we are helping to build His kingdom, to spread His love, and to fulfill the purpose He has given us.

So let us embrace this calling with courage, trusting that God has equipped us, enabled us, and empowered us to be His witnesses. Let us speak His truth with love, knowing that He is with us, that His Spirit is guiding us, and that His Word is powerful. Let us remember that every conversation, every testimony, and every act of kindness can be a step toward bringing someone closer to Him. Enabled by God, we can share the Gospel without fear, knowing that we are fulfilling the mission He has given us, and that we are part of His beautiful plan to bring hope, salvation, and life to a world in need.

Chapter 16 – Embraced

To be embraced by God means to be fully accepted, loved, and cherished as His child, a truth that brings comfort, peace, and joy to our hearts. John 1:12 tells us, "But as many as received him, to them gave he power to become the sons of God." This verse holds a powerful promise: when we receive Jesus, we are given the right to become God's children, welcomed fully into His family. We are not just invited to know about God; we are invited to know Him intimately, to experience His love, and to be embraced by Him in a relationship that changes everything. Being a child of God means that we are no longer strangers or outsiders; we are His, accepted completely and unconditionally. The love of God is unlike any human love; it doesn't depend on our achievements, our looks, or even our mistakes. God's embrace is pure, unwavering, and eternal, reaching us in our brokenness and lifting us up with grace.

When we are embraced by God, we are given a new identity. We are no longer defined by our past, our failures, or the labels that others may place on us. In God's family, we are called His beloved, His sons and daughters, precious and valuable in His sight. This embrace is not something we have to earn or prove; it is given to us freely because of His great love. When we come to Him, just as we are, He wraps us in His arms, assuring us that we belong, that we are safe, and that we are deeply loved. In a world where acceptance can often feel conditional or temporary, God's embrace offers us a love that is constant, unchanging, and complete. He accepts us fully, knowing every part of us, even the parts we may hide or struggle with. This acceptance is a gift, a reminder that we are always welcome in His presence, that we are His forever.

God's embrace also means that we are never alone. As His children, we have a constant companion, a loving Father who is always by our side, guiding us, comforting us, and encouraging us. When we face hardships, disappointments, or fears, we can rest in His embrace, knowing that He will carry us through. His love is a refuge, a safe place where we can find strength and hope, no matter what we are going through. Being embraced by God means we can bring all our worries, our questions, and our hurts to Him, knowing that He cares deeply for us. He listens to us, understands us, and meets us where we are. In His arms, we find peace, healing, and a sense of belonging that the world cannot offer. His embrace is like a shelter that protects us from the storms of life, reminding us that we are held securely in His hands.

This divine embrace also gives us purpose. As children of God, we are not only loved; we are called to live for Him, to reflect His love to those around us, and to share the hope we have found. God's embrace fills our hearts with love that overflows, enabling us to love others as He has loved us. We are given a mission to be His representatives on earth, to be the light in a dark world, and to bring the message of His love to those who are lost. His embrace transforms us, helping us to see ourselves and others through His eyes. We begin to live with confidence, knowing that our worth comes from being His children. This identity shapes our choices, our actions, and our relationships, as we seek to honor the One who has called us His own.

As we embrace God's love, we are empowered to let go of fear, guilt, and shame. We are reminded that we are forgiven, redeemed, and made new. His love covers our sins, heals our wounds, and gives us a fresh start. Each day, as we draw closer to Him, we experience the depth of His embrace, a love that goes beyond our understanding but meets every need of our hearts. This love is personal, intimate, and real, touching every part of our lives and filling us with a joy that endures. God's embrace teaches us that we are accepted not because of what we do, but because of who we are in Him. We are His children, chosen and beloved, called to live in the fullness of His grace.

In times of doubt or insecurity, we can look to God's promise in John 1:12 and remember that we are His. He has given us the power to become His sons and daughters, a truth that cannot be taken away. No matter what the world may say, God's Word assures us that we belong to Him, that we are precious in His sight, and that we are loved with an everlasting love. His embrace is a reminder that we are never out of reach, that His love pursues us, and that His grace is always available. This assurance gives us strength to face each day with hope, knowing that we are accepted, valued, and deeply loved.

God's embrace also brings us into a family, the body of Christ, where we find fellowship, support, and encouragement. As His children, we are connected to one another, sharing in the same love and mission. We are not alone in our journey; we have brothers and sisters who walk alongside us, lifting us up, praying for us, and encouraging us in our faith. This community is a gift from God, a reflection of His embrace, reminding us that we are part of something greater than ourselves. Together, we experience His love, grow in faith, and work to spread His message to a world in need.

Being embraced by God is a beautiful, life-changing gift. It fills us with peace, gives us a sense of belonging, and inspires us to live with purpose. We are His children, cherished and accepted, called to share His love and to walk in His ways. As we rest in His embrace, we are strengthened, renewed, and filled with joy. Let us live each day with the assurance that we are fully accepted as children of God, loved by a Father who will never let us go. His embrace is our refuge, our strength, and our hope, guiding us through every season and reminding us that we are His, now and forever.

Chapter 17 – Exemplary

To be exemplary as a follower of Christ means that we are called to be a living example of His love, grace, and truth in everything we do. In Matthew 5:16, Jesus says, "Let your light so shine before men, that they may see your good works." This verse reminds us that our lives are meant to reflect the light of Jesus, showing the world who He is through our actions, our words, and our hearts. Being an example of Christ's love isn't about seeking attention or praise; it's about living in such a way that others are drawn to the goodness of God. When we live as an example of Christ, we bring His light into a dark world, giving hope, kindness, and compassion to those who may never have experienced such love before. Our lives become a testament to the power of His love, a story of His grace, and a beacon that points others toward Him.

Being exemplary means that our actions speak louder than words, showing our faith through the way we treat others, the choices we make, and the integrity with which we live. It means loving our neighbors, forgiving those who hurt us, and serving without expecting anything in return. This kind of life is not always easy, but when we are rooted in God's love, He gives us the strength to be a light in the world. People around us are watching, noticing how we handle difficulties, how we respond to challenges, and how we treat others. Our lives have the power to make a difference, to inspire others, and to show them that there is a better way—a way of love, hope, and peace found only in Jesus.

Being an example of Christ's love means putting others first, showing kindness even when it's inconvenient, and offering grace in moments of conflict. It means letting God's love fill our hearts so completely that it overflows into every relationship, every conversation, and every action. We are called to be representatives of Jesus, reflecting His character, His humility, and His compassion. This call challenges us to rise above selfishness, to let go of anger, and to choose love, even when it's hard. It calls us to be patient, gentle, and forgiving, just as Christ is with us. When we strive to live like Jesus, we show others that His love is real, powerful, and life-changing. Our good works are not meant to glorify ourselves, but to point others to Him, to give them a glimpse of His love and to invite them to experience it for themselves.

An exemplary life also means living with integrity, being honest and true to our values even when no one is watching. It means being faithful in the small things, doing our best in every task, and treating everyone with respect and dignity. When we are faithful in the little things, God can use us for even greater purposes. Living as an example of Christ's love doesn't mean we are perfect, but it does mean that we are committed to growing, to seeking forgiveness when we fall short, and to letting God transform us day by day. Our weaknesses and failures don't disqualify us; instead, they remind us of our need for God's grace and help us to show others that His love is for everyone, no matter where they are in life.

This calling to be exemplary is also an invitation to find joy in serving others, to experience the fulfillment that comes from giving and caring. When we serve, when we help those in need, and when we reach out to the hurting, we are living out the heart of Jesus. He came not to be served, but to serve, and as His followers, we are called to do the same. Each act of kindness, each moment of compassion, and each choice to love over hate becomes a part of our testimony, a way of showing others the love of Christ. As we serve with a genuine heart, we not only bless others, but we also grow closer to God, becoming more like Him and discovering the joy of a life lived for others.

Being exemplary also means living with courage, standing up for what is right, and being willing to speak truth in a world that sometimes prefers lies. It means having the courage to be different, to live by God's standards even when it goes against the culture around us. This kind of life takes strength, but God promises to be with us, to guide us, and to give us the courage we need. When we stand firm in our faith, when we choose to live according to God's ways, we become a light that shines brightly, showing others that there is hope, there is truth, and there is a Savior who loves them.

As we strive to be exemplary, we must also remember that we do not have to do it alone. God's Spirit is with us, empowering us, guiding us, and helping us to live out His love. He gives us the patience, the kindness, and the wisdom we need to be His representatives. When we feel weak or discouraged, we can turn to Him, and He will strengthen us, reminding us of our purpose and filling us with His love. Living as an example of Christ's love is a journey, one that requires daily commitment, prayer, and a heart that is open to God's work. As we grow in our relationship with Him, He changes us, helping us to become more and more like Him, shining His light through us in ways we may not even realize.

Our lives are like a canvas, and as we live for Christ, He paints a picture of His love, hope, and grace for the world to see. We may never know the full impact of our example, but God sees every act of kindness, every moment of patience, and every choice to love. He uses our lives to reach others, to plant seeds of faith, and to bring His kingdom to earth. When we live as an example of Christ's love, we are fulfilling our purpose, bringing glory to God, and showing others the way to Him. Our light may be just one among many, but together, as the body of Christ, we shine brightly, illuminating a world that needs His love more than ever.

So let us embrace this calling to be exemplary, to let our light shine before men, that they may see our good works and glorify our Father in heaven. Let us live each day with purpose, knowing that God has chosen us to be His ambassadors, to represent His love, and to show the world who He is. As we live out His love, we become a part of His story, a story of redemption, hope, and grace. May our lives be a testament to His goodness, a reflection of His love, and a light that guides others to Him.

Chapter 18 – Engaged

To be engaged in our Christian walk means to be actively involved in serving and ministering to others, pouring out our hearts with dedication and passion as we live out our faith. In Romans 12:11, we are urged to be "Not slothful in business; fervent in spirit; serving the Lord." This verse reminds us that as followers of Christ, we are called to live with enthusiasm, not laziness, giving our best in everything we do as we serve God and others. Being engaged is more than just attending church on Sundays; it means living each day with purpose, seeing every moment as an opportunity to show God's love and to make a difference in the lives of those around us. Whether we're serving in our community, helping our families, volunteering in our church, or simply showing kindness to a stranger, every act of service reflects our love for God and our commitment to His kingdom. To be engaged means that we are not passive or indifferent but fully involved, ready to lend a helping hand, a listening ear, or an encouraging word whenever there is a need.

Engagement in ministry and service means that we are willing to step out of our comfort zones, to go the extra mile, and to give our time, energy, and resources to bless others. Jesus set the ultimate example of service, washing His disciples' feet, healing the sick, feeding the hungry, and ultimately giving His life for us. When we are engaged, we are following His footsteps, not seeking recognition or rewards but simply wanting to love as He loved. Serving others is an act of worship, a way of saying "thank you" to God for all He has done for us. Each time we reach out to someone in need, we are showing God's love in a tangible way, helping to build His kingdom on earth. Engaging in ministry allows us to see God working through us, using our hands, our words, and our hearts to touch lives and make a lasting impact. There is joy in being part of God's work, knowing that we are contributing to something bigger than ourselves.

When we are engaged in serving others, our lives become a witness to the power of God's love. People around us see our dedication, our kindness, and our commitment, and they are drawn to the source of our joy and strength—Jesus Christ. Being engaged means that we are willing to be God's hands and feet, to reach out to the lost, the hurting, and the lonely with compassion and care. It means being ready to share the Gospel, to offer a prayer, or simply to be present for someone in need. Our engagement in ministry is a reflection of our faith, a way of living out the love we have received from God. As we serve, we grow closer to Him, learning more about His heart and deepening our own faith. Each act of service strengthens our relationship with God, making us more like Him and allowing His love to flow through us.

Engagement in ministry also requires commitment and perseverance. There will be times when serving is challenging, when we feel tired, or when we face obstacles, but being engaged means that we stay faithful, trusting that God will give us the strength to continue. He sees every effort, every sacrifice, and every act of love, and He promises to bless our faithfulness. When we are engaged, we are part of a team, the body of Christ, working together to bring hope and healing to a world in need. Each person's role is important, and when we all come together, we create a powerful force for good, showing the world the love and unity that comes from knowing Christ. Being engaged in ministry is not a burden; it is a privilege, a chance to participate in God's work and to make a difference that will last for eternity.

To be engaged is to live with a servant's heart, always looking for ways to bless others and to glorify God. It means putting others before ourselves, seeking to lift them up, and showing them the same grace and mercy that God has shown us. This kind of engagement fills our lives with purpose and meaning, reminding us that we are here not just for ourselves but for something greater. Every time we serve, we are planting seeds of hope, faith, and love in the hearts of those around us. Some of these seeds may take time to grow, but God promises that our labor is never in vain. He is the one who brings the increase, using our efforts to accomplish His will. Being engaged in serving others fills our hearts with joy and gratitude, knowing that we are part of His kingdom and that our actions can have an eternal impact.

Serving others also deepens our own faith, as we see God's love in action. Each time we reach out, we experience His presence, His guidance, and His strength. Being engaged in ministry is a journey of faith, where we learn to rely on God, to trust in His timing, and to see His hand at work in our lives. When we serve, we are reminded of God's goodness, and we are filled with gratitude for the privilege of being used by Him. Our engagement in ministry helps us to grow, to stretch beyond our limits, and to discover gifts and abilities we may not have known we had. God equips us for every good work, giving us the tools we need to serve Him effectively. As we engage with others, we become more compassionate, more patient, and more understanding, learning to see people through God's eyes.

Being engaged in serving others also means that we are part of a community, the body of Christ, working together to fulfill God's mission. We are never alone in this work; we have brothers and sisters who stand with us, encourage us, and pray for us. This community strengthens us, helping us to stay focused, to stay motivated, and to keep moving forward. When we are engaged in ministry, we are building relationships, creating bonds of fellowship that lift us up and remind us that we are all in this together. Serving together brings joy, camaraderie, and a sense of belonging, knowing that we are part of God's family, working side by side for His glory.

In every act of service, big or small, we are fulfilling the calling that God has placed on our lives. Being engaged in ministry means that we live with our hearts open, ready to be used by God, and willing to make a difference wherever we are. It is a commitment to live each day with purpose, to see each person as valuable, and to seize every opportunity to share God's love. This engagement fills our lives with joy, knowing that we are living out our faith and making a difference for His kingdom. As we stay engaged, God continues to mold us, shape us, and use us in ways that we may not even fully understand. He is working through us, using our lives to bring His light to a world that desperately needs it.

Let us be engaged, fervent in spirit, and dedicated to serving the Lord, knowing that each act of love, each moment of compassion, and each word of encouragement has the power to change lives. May we serve with joy, with dedication, and with a heart that reflects the love of Christ in all that we do.

Chapter 19 - Enabled for Endurance

To be enabled for endurance means that God empowers us to stay strong, to keep our faith, and to persevere through every challenge, no matter how hard the journey may seem. In Hebrews 12:1, we are encouraged to "run with patience the race that is set before us." This verse reminds us that life is like a race, filled with obstacles, twists, and turns, but God calls us to keep going, to stay on course, and to remain steadfast in our faith. Endurance is not just about surviving; it's about running this race with purpose, trusting that God is with us every step of the way. He doesn't expect us to do it alone; He gives us strength, courage, and the support we need to keep moving forward. When we feel tired, weak, or discouraged, God renews our spirit, lifting us up and reminding us that we are not alone. Being enabled for endurance means that we are equipped to face life's trials with a faith that does not waver, a hope that does not fade, and a love that keeps us going, no matter what.

Life's journey is filled with moments that test our strength and our faith. We may encounter struggles, losses, disappointments, and moments of deep uncertainty. But God, in His love, gives us the ability to endure, to hold onto His promises, and to keep our eyes on Him. Just as a runner stays focused on the finish line, we are called to keep our focus on Jesus, the author and finisher of our faith. He knows the path we are on; He has walked it before, and He promises to guide us through. Each step we take, even when it's difficult, brings us closer to Him, strengthens our character, and builds our resilience. Endurance is a gift that grows as we trust God, lean on His strength, and remember that He is working in us and through us. Every trial we endure becomes a testimony of His faithfulness, a story of His grace, and a reminder that we are never left to struggle on our own.

Being enabled for endurance also means that we can face challenges with patience and perseverance. Patience doesn't mean waiting passively; it means continuing to move forward, even when the journey is long and the obstacles are many. It's about having the courage to keep going, to take one step at a time, and to trust that God's timing is perfect. He knows the end from the beginning, and He uses each part of our journey to shape us, to teach us, and to prepare us for what lies ahead. God's timing may not always match our own desires or plans, but He sees the bigger picture, and He knows what we need in order to grow and fulfill His purpose for our lives. As we endure with patience, we learn to let go of our own control, to surrender our fears, and to trust that God is guiding us every step of the way.

Endurance is also about holding onto hope, even when things seem impossible. God's promises give us the strength to face each day with faith, knowing that He is faithful and that His plans for us are good. The challenges we face can feel overwhelming, but with God's help, we are able to stand firm, to resist despair, and to keep believing that He is with us. Our endurance grows as we rely on His Word, filling our minds and hearts with His truth, His promises, and His love. When we are grounded in God's truth, we are not easily shaken. His Word becomes our anchor, keeping us steady in the storms of life, reminding us that He is our refuge, our strength, and our ever-present help in times of trouble.

Being enabled for endurance also means that we are part of a community of believers who support and encourage each other. We don't have to run this race alone; God has given us brothers and sisters in Christ who walk alongside us, lifting us up in prayer, sharing our burdens, and cheering us on. The body of Christ is a source of strength, a reminder that we are all running this race together, and that we can draw encouragement from one another. When one of us stumbles, the others are there to help us back up, to remind us of God's promises, and to encourage us to keep going. This fellowship is a gift from God, a source of strength, and a reminder that we are never truly alone. Together, we press on, each of us contributing our strength, our faith, and our love to help one another endure.

God's enabling power gives us the courage to face every season of life with confidence, knowing that He is with us. When we are weary, He renews our strength; when we are discouraged, He fills us with hope; when we are afraid, He gives us courage. His Spirit lives within us, empowering us, guiding us, and helping us to endure. No matter how difficult the path may seem, God's presence gives us peace, reminding us that He will never leave us nor forsake us. He is our constant companion, our source of strength, and our greatest encourager. When we feel like giving up, we can turn to Him, and He will lift us up, filling us with the power to keep moving forward.

Endurance also helps us to grow in our relationship with God, as each trial we face becomes an opportunity to rely on Him more deeply. Our faith is strengthened through every challenge, as we learn to trust His goodness, His faithfulness, and His love. The struggles we endure teach us humility, patience, and resilience, shaping our character and helping us to become more like Christ. God uses these experiences to refine us, to deepen our dependence on Him, and to draw us closer to His heart. As we endure, we come to know Him in ways we could not have known otherwise, discovering His strength, His wisdom, and His unfailing love.

To be enabled for endurance is to live with hope, courage, and faith, knowing that God is with us every step of the way. It is a reminder that our journey is not in vain, that each struggle has a purpose, and that God is working all things together for our good. We are called to run this race with patience, to keep pressing on, and to trust that God's grace is sufficient for every challenge we face. His power is made perfect in our weakness, and He promises to carry us through. Let us embrace this gift of endurance, knowing that God has empowered us to remain steadfast in faith, to overcome every obstacle, and to finish this race strong.

Chapter 20 – Empathetic

To be empathetic as a follower of Christ means to have a heart that cares deeply, to feel the struggles and joys of others as if they were our own, and to be moved with compassion in a world that often overlooks pain and suffering. Colossians 3:12 calls us to "Put on therefore... bowels of mercies, kindness, humbleness of mind, meekness, longsuffering." This verse reminds us that, as God's chosen people, we are to be clothed in compassion and humility, approaching others with a spirit of gentleness and patience. Empathy is about putting ourselves in someone else's shoes, understanding their emotions, and responding with genuine kindness and love. It's about going beyond sympathy, which is feeling sorry for someone, to truly sharing in their experience. God calls us to be empathetic because He knows that love, shown through compassion, has the power to heal, uplift, and comfort those who are hurting.

Being empathetic reflects the heart of Jesus, who was moved with compassion everywhere He went. He felt the needs of the people around Him deeply, reaching out to the sick, the poor, the lost, and the broken with love and mercy. When we are empathetic, we are following in His footsteps, showing others the same kindness and care that He has shown us. This kind of love doesn't just happen; it grows as we open our hearts to God and allow His Spirit to fill us with His love. Empathy requires humility because it asks us to set aside our own concerns and focus on the needs of others. It requires a gentle spirit, willing to listen and to offer support, even when we may not fully understand what someone else is going through. Empathy invites us to be present for others, to be a shoulder to lean on, and to be a source of encouragement.

When we are empathetic, we reflect God's love in a powerful way. People see that we care not just with words but with actions, and they feel valued and understood. In a world that often rushes past the pain of others, empathy is a gift that slows us down, that reminds us to look into the eyes of those around us and to see them as God does. This care for others grows as we learn to love as Christ loved, putting on "bowels of mercies," letting our hearts be softened by the love of God. Empathy allows us to connect deeply with others, building relationships that are grounded in trust, respect, and genuine concern. When we show empathy, we become vessels of God's comfort, bringing hope and encouragement to those who may feel alone or forgotten.

Empathy is not always easy; it asks us to open ourselves up, to share in others' burdens, and to sometimes feel the weight of their struggles. Yet, in doing so, we fulfill one of the greatest commandments—to love our neighbor as ourselves. We become a reflection of God's love, His kindness, and His care. God gives us the strength to be empathetic, to remain patient, and to offer kindness, even when it's challenging. His Spirit works in us, helping us to see beyond ourselves, to become aware of the needs around us, and to respond with a heart of compassion. Empathy allows us to be the hands and feet of Jesus, reaching out to those who are in pain, bringing comfort, and sharing His love in a way that words alone cannot do.

When we are empathetic, we also grow in humility, realizing that each person's journey is unique and valuable. We learn not to judge but to accept others where they are, offering love without conditions. Empathy teaches us to be patient, to listen more than we speak, and to offer support in whatever way we can. As we practice empathy, we draw closer to God, seeing people through His eyes and feeling His love for them. This understanding helps us to be more forgiving, more compassionate, and more willing to serve others. It reminds us that we are all part of God's family, called to support one another, to bear one another's burdens, and to lift each other up in love.

Empathy also builds a sense of unity within the body of Christ. As we share in each other's joys and sorrows, we grow stronger together, supporting one another through life's ups and downs. When we are empathetic, we become a source of strength for our brothers and sisters in Christ, showing them that they are not alone, that their struggles matter, and that they are loved. This unity is a testimony to the world of God's love, as people see the compassion and care we have for each other. Empathy brings healing, not only to those we serve but to ourselves as well. It helps us to grow in love, to develop a deeper understanding of others, and to see the beauty of God's creation in every person we meet.

God's call to empathy is an invitation to love as He loves, to be a light in a world that often overlooks those who are hurting. It challenges us to go beyond ourselves, to reach out with open hearts, and to offer compassion without expecting anything in return. Each time we show empathy, we are planting seeds of kindness, building bridges, and creating a space where others feel safe and valued. God equips us for this call, giving us a heart that is tender, a spirit that is patient, and a love that is strong. He helps us to carry this empathy into our daily lives, making a difference wherever we go, showing the world that His love is real, and that it is for everyone.

Let us embrace this calling to be empathetic, putting on kindness, humility, and patience as we serve others. May we be a reflection of Christ's love, a source of comfort, and a light of hope to all those we meet. As we live with empathy, we fulfill God's command to love, bringing His healing and grace to a world in need. Empathy is a powerful way to share God's love, a reminder that we are all connected, and that each of us has the ability to make a difference, one act of compassion at a time. Let us be empathetic, for in doing so, we draw others closer to the love of Christ.

Chapter 21 – Exhorted

To be exhorted in our walk with God means to be encouraged, strengthened, and called to remain faithful and true to His Word, always pressing forward in His love and purpose. In Hebrews 10:24, we are reminded, "And let us consider one another to provoke unto love and to good works." This verse calls us to lift one another up, to inspire each other to live for God, and to keep pursuing what is right, loving, and true. Being exhorted is not just about receiving encouragement; it is also about offering it, helping others stay strong in their faith and reminding them that they are not alone. We are called to be a support system for one another, to spur each other on when the journey gets tough, and to gently remind one another of the beauty and power of God's promises. Life can be challenging, filled with moments of doubt, fear, and hardship. But God, in His love, places us in a community of believers where we can build each other up, sharing hope, strength, and courage so that we all remain steadfast in our journey of faith.

Exhortation helps us stay focused on God's truth, especially when we are tempted to stray or when the world tries to pull us away from His path. When we exhort each other, we remind one another of God's goodness, His faithfulness, and His promises. This encouragement is like a spark that reignites our faith, helping us to keep going, even when things seem difficult. Exhortation helps us to remember why we believe, who we are in Christ, and the hope that we have in Him. It's like a gentle push forward, a reminder that we have a purpose and that God is with us every step of the way. When we feel weak, God uses others to encourage us, to speak words of life, and to lift us up. And when others around us are struggling, God calls us to be that voice of encouragement, offering them the same hope and strength that we have received.

Exhortation is more than just positive words; it's a reminder of our calling to live in love and to do good works. It challenges us to rise above our struggles and to choose faith, even when things are hard. When we encourage one another to love and good works, we are fulfilling God's command to care for each other, to be a light in the world, and to show His love through our actions. Our lives become a testimony of His grace, a reflection of His kindness, and an example for others to follow. Exhortation reminds us that our faith is not just for us alone; it is meant to be shared, to inspire others, and to make a difference in the lives of those around us. As we encourage one another, we grow in unity, supporting each other in our weaknesses, celebrating each other's strengths, and helping each other to stay focused on what truly matters.

Through exhortation, we learn to persevere, to stand firm in God's truth, and to keep our eyes on Jesus. Life may try to discourage us, to fill us with doubt, or to distract us from our calling. But with the encouragement of our brothers and sisters in Christ, we are reminded to stay strong, to keep moving forward, and to trust in God's plan. Exhortation helps us to find joy in our journey, to celebrate the small victories, and to hold onto hope, even in the face of trials. It is a gift from God, a tool He uses to strengthen our faith and to remind us that we are never alone. When we encourage others, we are also blessed, as we see God working through us to bring comfort, courage, and hope to those who need it.

Being exhorted by others is like receiving a fresh breath of life, a boost that helps us to keep running our race with endurance. God knows that we need each other, that we are stronger together, and that encouragement is essential for our spiritual growth. When we come together to lift each other up, we create a community of love, trust, and support, where each person feels valued and cared for. Exhortation builds a foundation of faith that can withstand the storms of life, as we remind one another of the unchanging truth of God's Word. Together, we are stronger, more resilient, and more able to face the challenges that come our way. Exhortation is a powerful expression of God's love, a way of saying, "You are not alone. God is with you, and so am I."

This calling to exhort each other is a responsibility, but it is also a joy. As we encourage others, we see the difference it makes, how a simple word of kindness or a reminder of God's love can lift someone's spirit and renew their faith. We realize that God can use us, even in small ways, to be a blessing, to bring light, and to help others see the beauty of God's truth. Exhortation calls us to be attentive to the needs of those around us, to listen with compassion, and to speak with wisdom and love. It reminds us that each of us has a role in building up the body of Christ, helping each other to grow, to heal, and to find strength in God.

Exhorting others also helps us to stay connected to God, as we rely on His wisdom and strength to be an encouragement. It deepens our faith, as we see His Word come alive in our lives and in the lives of those we encourage. As we exhort one another, we are reminded of God's promises, His guidance, and His faithfulness. This mutual encouragement strengthens our relationship with Him, drawing us closer to His heart and helping us to become more like Christ. We become instruments of His peace, His love, and His grace, reaching out to those in need and helping them to see that God is always with them.

Let us embrace this calling to exhort one another, to provoke each other unto love and good works. Let us be a source of strength, a light of hope, and a voice of encouragement for those around us. In doing so, we fulfill God's command to love one another, to build each other up, and to live out our faith in a way that brings glory to Him. May our lives be filled with encouragement, as we walk together in faith, helping each other to stay true to God's truth and to continue on the path He has set before us.

Chapter 22 – Enlisted

To be enlisted in God's mission on earth is a powerful calling, a reminder that we have been chosen and set apart to live for a purpose greater than ourselves. 2 Timothy 2:4 says, "No man that warreth entangleth himself with the affairs of this life." This verse speaks to the focus and dedication required of someone enlisted in God's mission. When we are enlisted by God, we are like soldiers in His service, called to be fully committed, ready to follow His lead, and willing to put His will above our own desires and distractions. God's mission on earth is to bring His love, truth, and salvation to all people, and He has chosen us to be a part of that mission. It's an incredible privilege, but also a serious responsibility, one that asks us to be courageous, faithful, and willing to let go of anything that holds us back from wholeheartedly serving Him.

Being enlisted by God means we have a new identity; we are no longer simply living for ourselves but are now ambassadors of His love and grace. This calling changes the way we live, the way we think, and the choices we make. When we are enlisted, we realize that each moment of our lives can be used to glorify God and to share His message of hope with others. We become representatives of His kingdom, bringing light into dark places, spreading kindness, and showing compassion. God doesn't call us to this mission because of anything we have done; it's not based on our talents or our strengths. He calls us because of His love for us and His desire to use us as vessels of His grace. Through our lives, others can see the love of Christ, feel His compassion, and come to know His truth.

Being enlisted requires focus and determination, a commitment to put God's mission above the temporary distractions of this world. This doesn't mean we ignore our daily responsibilities, but rather that we keep our priorities centered on God's purpose. We are called to live with an eternal perspective, to remember that our time here on earth is limited and that what we do for

ENABLED- LIVING GOD'S PURPOSE WITH POWER

God's kingdom has everlasting value. Every act of kindness, every word of encouragement, every moment spent serving others is part of God's mission. Being enlisted means that we are willing to sacrifice, to step out of our comfort zones, and to say "yes" to God, even when it's difficult. It's about surrendering our lives to His plan and trusting that He knows what is best.

God gives us the strength we need to fulfill this mission. He equips us with His Spirit, guiding us, empowering us, and giving us the courage to stand firm in our faith. When we feel weak or unsure, He is there to lift us up, to remind us that we are not alone, and to fill us with His strength. Being enlisted by God is not something we do in our own power; it is His Spirit working in us, helping us to live out His purpose with boldness and faith. God calls us to stay focused, to avoid the distractions and temptations that try to pull us away from Him. Just as a soldier keeps his mind on the mission, we are to keep our eyes on Jesus, staying close to Him, and allowing His Word to be our guide.

To be enlisted in God's mission also means that we are part of a larger family, the body of Christ, working together to fulfill His purpose on earth. Each of us has a unique role to play, and when we come together, we create a powerful force for good. We support each other, encourage each other, and stand together as we share God's love with the world. Being enlisted means that we are never alone; we have brothers and sisters in Christ who walk alongside us, who pray for us, and who help us to stay strong. Together, we are the hands and feet of Jesus, reaching out to those in need, bringing hope to the hopeless, and sharing the Gospel with those who are lost. God's mission is bigger than any one of us, but together, with His Spirit guiding us, we can make a difference.

Being enlisted also means living with purpose, knowing that each day is an opportunity to serve God and to make an impact for His kingdom. It's about waking up each morning with a sense of mission, ready to love, to give, and to be a light in the world. When we are enlisted, we are part of something far greater than ourselves, a mission that has eternal significance. This purpose gives our lives meaning, filling us with joy, hope, and a desire to see God's love reach every corner of the earth. God has chosen us, not because we are perfect, but because He loves us and wants to use us to share His message of hope. Each of us has a unique story, a unique way of reflecting God's love, and He calls us to be faithful in sharing that with others.

As we go about our daily lives, being enlisted in God's mission means that we look for opportunities to serve, to be kind, and to share the truth of the Gospel. Whether it's through a conversation with a friend, helping someone in need, or simply showing compassion, each moment can be a part of God's mission. We don't need to have all the answers or be perfect; we just need to be willing, open, and ready to let God work through us. Being enlisted means saying, "Here I am, Lord, use me." It's about being available, trusting that God can use our lives, even in small ways, to bring others closer to Him.

To be enlisted in God's mission is both a challenge and a blessing. It calls us to live differently, to let go of the distractions that don't matter, and to focus on what does. It's a life of purpose, of serving others, and of loving with the love of Christ. As we live out this mission, we find joy in knowing that we are fulfilling the purpose God has for us. We are His representatives, His ambassadors, sharing His love, His truth, and His hope with the world. This mission is not always easy, but God promises to be with us, to give us strength, and to guide us each step of the way. Being enlisted means we are part of God's beautiful plan, chosen to make a difference, and blessed to carry His message of salvation to all people.

Let us embrace this calling to be enlisted, living each day with purpose, focus, and a heart that is fully committed to God's mission on earth. We are His servants, His soldiers, and His children, working together to bring His kingdom to a world in need.

Chapter 23 – Entrenched

To be entrenched in the truth of God's Word means to be firmly grounded, deeply rooted, and unshakeable in our faith, drawing our strength and nourishment from the promises of God. Psalm 1:3 tells us, "And he shall be like a tree planted by the rivers of water." This image of a tree by the riverside shows us a life that is steady, secure, and continuously refreshed by God's living water. Just as a tree planted near a river has deep roots that reach down for the water it needs, being entrenched in God's Word means that we are constantly drawing from the wisdom, love, and strength found in Scripture. When we root ourselves in God's truth, we become steady and resilient, able to withstand life's challenges because we are grounded in something greater than ourselves. God's Word becomes our foundation, our anchor, and our source of hope, keeping us strong and steady, no matter what storms may come our way.

Living a life entrenched in God's Word means that we are not easily swayed by the opinions, pressures, or worries of the world. We know who we are and Whose we are, and that knowledge keeps us secure. Just as a tree with deep roots is able to stand firm even in strong winds, we too can stand firm in our faith when we are deeply rooted in the truth of Scripture. God's Word gives us the strength to resist temptation, the courage to face difficulties, and the wisdom to make the right choices. Being entrenched means that we are committed to knowing and living out God's Word, making it a part of our daily lives, so that His truth shapes our thoughts, our actions, and our character. The more we dig into His Word, the deeper our roots grow, and the more stable we become, able to remain steadfast even when life tries to shake us.

Being entrenched in God's truth also means that we are constantly nourished and refreshed by His promises. Just as a tree by the river never lacks water, our souls never lack hope, peace, or joy when we stay close to God's Word. His promises give us life, filling us with strength, comfort, and guidance every day. When we are tired, His Word renews us; when we are uncertain, His Word directs us; and when we are weak, His Word strengthens us. Being entrenched means that we continually turn to Scripture for the answers, the encouragement, and the wisdom we need. God's Word becomes our constant source of life, giving us what we need to grow, to bear fruit, and to shine His light in the world.

Living a life entrenched in God's Word also keeps us grounded in truth, protecting us from being misled by false teachings or worldly lies. When we know God's Word deeply, we are able to recognize what is true and what is not, and we are able to hold onto His promises even when others try to pull us away. This kind of life is rooted in conviction, knowing that God's truth never changes and that His promises are always faithful. Being entrenched means that we know His Word by heart, that we carry it with us wherever we go, and that it becomes our guide in every situation. God's truth is unchanging, and when we are rooted in that truth, we become unshakeable, standing firm in our faith no matter what challenges we face.

Entrenching ourselves in God's Word also helps us to grow in maturity and wisdom. Just as a tree grows taller and stronger over time, our faith grows deeper and more resilient as we spend time in Scripture. God's Word teaches us how to live, how to love, and how to serve others. It gives us insight into His character, helping us to understand His love, His grace, and His mercy. Each time we read the Bible, we learn something new, something that helps us to grow and to become more like Christ. Being entrenched in God's Word means that we are constantly learning, constantly growing, and constantly being transformed by His truth. This growth is a beautiful journey, one that fills us with purpose, joy, and a sense of belonging.

Being entrenched in God's truth also means that we become a source of encouragement and strength for others. Just as a tree provides shade, shelter, and fruit, our lives can provide support, comfort, and guidance to those around us. When we are deeply rooted in God's Word, we are able to share His truth with others, offering them hope and encouragement in their own journeys. We become a blessing to those around us, a steady presence that reflects God's love, peace, and grace. Our faith becomes a light in the darkness, a testimony of God's goodness, and an example of what it means to live a life grounded in His truth. By staying rooted in God's Word, we are equipped to help others find their own strength, hope, and peace in Him.

Entrenched in God's Word, we learn to trust Him more fully, to rely on His promises, and to find joy in His presence. We discover that His Word is alive, speaking to us, guiding us, and comforting us in every season of life. Just as a tree's roots grow deeper over time, our relationship with God deepens as we spend time in His Word, learning to hear His voice and to follow His lead. This rootedness gives us confidence, not in ourselves, but in God's unchanging love and faithfulness. Being entrenched means that we are held secure by God's promises, that our lives are built on the solid foundation of His truth, and that we can face anything with courage, knowing that He is with us.

To be entrenched in God's Word is to live a life of purpose, strength, and peace. It means that our hearts are anchored in His truth, that our minds are filled with His wisdom, and that our souls are nourished by His presence. When we are deeply rooted in Scripture, we find that our lives are transformed, filled with love, joy, and a desire to serve God in everything we do. Let us commit to being entrenched in God's Word, letting it shape us, guide us, and keep us strong, so that we may be like a tree planted by the rivers of water, bearing fruit for His glory, and standing firm in our faith, no matter what.

Chapter 24 - Encompassed by Grace

To be encompassed by grace means to be surrounded and supported by God's deep, unfailing love in every part of our lives. In 2 Corinthians 12:9, we find the powerful words, "My grace is sufficient for thee," reminding us that God's grace is all we need, more than enough to carry us through any trial, fear, or weakness. His grace is like a shield around us, protecting, comforting, and giving us strength when we feel weak. God's grace isn't something we have to earn; it's a gift, freely given because of His love for us. Being encompassed by grace means that no matter where we go, what we face, or how we may struggle, God's love is there, holding us steady. When life feels overwhelming or we feel like we don't have the strength to keep going, His grace surrounds us, whispering that we are not alone and that He is with us. God's grace means He accepts us just as we are, but loves us too much to leave us that way. His grace lifts us up, encouraging us to keep pressing forward, reminding us that His strength is made perfect in our weakness.

Living encompassed by grace changes how we see ourselves and how we handle challenges. We begin to realize that we are valuable, loved, and cherished, not because of anything we have done, but because of who God is. His grace surrounds us like an endless ocean, washing over us with peace, patience, and mercy. When we make mistakes, His grace is there to forgive us and to help us start fresh. When we fall, His grace picks us up, dusts us off, and gives us the courage to try again. No matter how many times we stumble, God's grace is always there, a constant reminder that His love for us never fails. Being encompassed by grace means that we don't have to live in guilt, fear, or shame. Instead, we can rest in the assurance that God's love covers all our faults, that His forgiveness is real, and that He sees us as His beloved children.

God's grace is not only a shield around us but also a source of strength within us. His grace empowers us to face difficulties with courage, to love others even when it's hard, and to keep moving forward when life is challenging. It is His grace that helps us forgive, even when we've been hurt deeply, and it is His grace that gives us patience and peace in times of waiting. Every day, we draw from the well of His grace, finding the strength to live in a way that honors Him, to love with His love, and to walk in His truth. We don't have to rely on our own strength because God's grace is all we need. His grace fills the gaps in our abilities, giving us wisdom when we are confused, calm in the face of anxiety, and hope when things seem hopeless. Being encompassed by grace means that we can trust God to provide everything we need, exactly when we need it.

When we are encompassed by God's grace, we also learn to extend grace to others. Just as God loves us unconditionally, even when we fall short, we are called to show that same love to those around us. His grace teaches us to be patient, to forgive, and to care for others with compassion. Living in His grace changes our hearts, helping us to be more like Jesus, who showed kindness to everyone He met. As we grow in grace, we become a reflection of God's love, a source of encouragement and strength for those who may feel alone or burdened. We become vessels of His grace, showing others that God's love is real and that His grace is available to all. This grace is a reminder that we are part of something bigger than ourselves, a family of believers called to live in love, support, and unity.

Being encompassed by grace also brings peace and joy. When we truly understand that God's grace is sufficient, we can let go of the burdens we carry, trusting that He is in control. We don't have to strive or struggle to earn His love; His grace already surrounds us, like a warm embrace that never lets go. Knowing that His grace is enough allows us to breathe deeply, to live freely, and to find joy in each day. We can wake up each morning with confidence, knowing that God's grace will meet us in whatever we face. Whether we are celebrating victories or enduring hardships, His grace is there, steady and unchanging, a foundation that keeps us grounded. This grace gives us hope, reminding us that no matter what tomorrow holds, God's love will be there, unshaken and unwavering.

Living in the embrace of God's grace transforms how we respond to life's challenges. Instead of feeling defeated by setbacks, we remember that God's grace is bigger than any obstacle. When life feels like too much, we can lean into His grace, knowing that He is our strength and that His love will see us through. Being encompassed by grace doesn't mean we won't face hard times, but it means that we never face them alone. God's grace is like a shelter in a storm, a safe place where we can find comfort, rest, and renewed strength. We can run to His grace whenever we need help, comfort, or peace, trusting that His love will always be enough.

In every season of life, God's grace surrounds us, supporting us, guiding us, and reminding us that we are His. Whether we are walking through joyful moments or painful trials, His grace is there, a constant presence that fills our lives with hope. To be encompassed by grace is to live with the confidence that God's love is all-encompassing, that nothing can separate us from Him, and that His mercy and kindness are new every morning. His grace is a daily gift, a reminder of His promises, and a sign of His faithfulness. As we walk in His grace, we learn to trust Him more, to rely on His love, and to rest in the peace that only He can give.

God's grace is a precious gift, a blessing that surrounds us every day. It is the reassurance that we are never out of reach of His love, that no matter where we are, He is there, holding us, lifting us up, and reminding us that we are cherished. His grace is like a never-ending river, always flowing, always available, and always enough. To be encompassed by grace is to live with hope, courage, and a heart full of gratitude, knowing that God's love surrounds us, sustains us, and strengthens us, now and forever.

Chapter 25 - Enabled for Eternity

To be enabled for eternity means to have the incredible assurance of everlasting life through Jesus Christ, a gift that changes everything about how we live, think, and hope. In John 10:28, Jesus promises, "And I give unto them eternal life; and they shall never perish." This verse gives us a powerful promise, one that fills our hearts with peace and joy. Jesus Himself assures us that we are held in His hands, and nothing can take us from His grasp. Eternal life is not just a future promise; it's a reality that begins the moment we place our faith in Jesus. We are enabled for eternity, equipped to live forever with God, and secure in the knowledge that our lives have meaning and purpose beyond the temporary things of this world. Knowing we have eternal life gives us a deep, abiding hope, one that goes beyond the struggles and trials of this life. It means that no matter what we face here, something far greater is waiting for us—a home in heaven, a place in God's presence, and a joy that will never end.

Eternal life is the greatest gift God could give, offered freely to us through the sacrifice of Jesus. He died and rose again so that we might live forever with Him, breaking the power of sin and death over our lives. This assurance of eternity is something we can hold onto in every season of life, especially in moments of fear, doubt, or loss. When we feel uncertain or afraid, God's promise of eternal life reminds us that He is in control, that He has a plan for us, and that nothing can separate us from His love. Being enabled for eternity fills us with a peace that passes all understanding, a peace that tells us that even when this life ends, it is not the end for us. We have a future that is secure, a place in God's kingdom, and a hope that will never fade.

Knowing that we are enabled for eternity changes the way we see life. It gives us courage, knowing that God is with us and that we are part of His eternal story. Every choice we make, every act of love, and every moment of faithfulness has eternal significance. We are not just living for today; we are living for eternity, storing up treasures in heaven, and making an impact that will last forever. This assurance also gives us strength in hard times, for we know that our present sufferings are only temporary, a small part of a much larger picture. When we are faced with pain, loss, or uncertainty, we can find comfort in God's promise of eternal life, knowing that one day He will wipe away every tear, and there will be no more death, sorrow, or pain.

Being enabled for eternity also means that we live with purpose, knowing that our lives are meant to reflect God's love and to share His truth with others. God calls us to be ambassadors of His kingdom, to show others the hope of eternal life, and to be lights in a world that often seems dark. As we live with the knowledge of eternity, we are reminded that every person we meet is someone God loves, someone He desires to bring into His kingdom. Our lives become a testimony of His grace, a beacon of hope, and a message of the joy that awaits those who trust in Jesus. This eternal perspective helps us to focus on what truly matters, to let go of temporary concerns, and to invest our time, love, and energy into things that will last forever.

God's promise of eternal life gives us a confidence that nothing in this world can shake. We know that we belong to Him, that we are His children, and that our future is secure. This assurance gives us boldness to live for Him, to share His message, and to stand firm in our faith, no matter what challenges we face. Being enabled for eternity means that we do not have to fear death, for Jesus has conquered it. Instead, we can look forward with hope, knowing that death is not the end but the beginning of a new and glorious life with our Savior. This knowledge fills our hearts with joy, even in the midst of sorrow, for we know that we will see our loved ones again, that we will dwell in the presence of God, and that we will experience a joy and peace beyond anything we can imagine.

As we live with the assurance of eternal life, we also experience God's presence here and now, for eternity begins the moment we accept Jesus as our Savior. We are already part of His kingdom, already living in His grace, and already experiencing the peace that comes from being His. This assurance of eternal life transforms our lives, giving us a sense of security, purpose, and joy that nothing else can provide. We are empowered to live boldly, to love deeply, and to serve faithfully, knowing that our lives have eternal significance. We are enabled to rise above fear, to walk in faith, and to trust in God's promises, for we know that He is preparing a place for us, a place where we will dwell with Him forever.

God's gift of eternal life is a reminder of His incredible love for us. He wants us to be with Him forever, to share in His joy, and to experience His love without end. This eternal life is not something we can earn; it is a gift, given freely through Jesus' sacrifice. All we have to do is accept it, to trust in Him, and to receive the life He offers. When we are enabled for eternity, we are set free from the chains of fear, doubt, and uncertainty. We know that our lives are held in His hands, that our future is secure, and that nothing can separate us from His love. This assurance gives us peace, joy, and a heart full of gratitude, for we know that God has chosen us, called us, and prepared a place for us in His kingdom.

Living with the assurance of eternity helps us to stay focused on what truly matters. We are reminded to love, to forgive, to show kindness, and to live in a way that honors God. We are called to be a light in the world, to share the hope we have, and to live as people who are not afraid of the future. As we keep our eyes on eternity, we are able to face each day with confidence, knowing that we are part of something far greater than ourselves. We are part of God's eternal plan, chosen to bring His love and truth to the world. This knowledge fills our hearts with joy, for we know that our lives are meaningful, our future is secure, and our hope is unshakable.

God's promise of eternal life is a treasure, a blessing, and a hope that fills us with peace. It is a reminder that we are never alone, that God is with us, and that our lives are held in His loving hands. We are enabled for eternity, called to live with joy, faith, and a heart that trusts in His promises. Let us live each day with the assurance that we are His, that our future is secure, and that we are part of His eternal kingdom, now and forever.

Chapter 26 - Encircled by Protection

To be encircled by God's protection means to be surrounded and safeguarded by His powerful and loving presence, every moment of every day. Psalm 91:4 beautifully says, "He shall cover thee with his feathers, and under his wings shalt thou trust." This verse paints a comforting picture of God as a caring protector, much like a mother bird who shelters her young under her wings, providing warmth, safety, and assurance. God's protection is a shield around us, a covering that guards us from harm and reassures us when we feel afraid. Just as a bird's wings wrap securely around its offspring, God's embrace holds us tightly, promising that He will never leave nor forsake us. Being encircled by His protection doesn't mean we won't face challenges or storms, but it means we have a powerful, loving Father who goes before us, stands beside us, and watches over us in all circumstances. His protection is constant and unchanging, no matter where we are or what we face, because His love is steadfast, and His promises are true.

God's protection gives us peace, even when the world around us is filled with chaos and fear. When we are encircled by His presence, we can find rest in His strength, knowing that He is greater than anything that threatens us. His Word tells us that He is our refuge and fortress, a safe place where we can run whenever we feel overwhelmed or in danger. This promise doesn't mean that difficulties won't come, but it assures us that we are never alone in those moments. God is our defender, our shield, and our strong tower. He stands between us and the forces that try to harm us, blocking their path and keeping us secure. His protection means that no weapon formed against us shall prosper, for He is the mighty God who fights for His children.

Being encircled by God's protection also means that we are guided by His wisdom and held by His hand. As we walk through life, we don't have to rely on our own understanding or strength because God is with us, directing our steps and lighting our path. His presence goes before us, preparing the way and keeping us safe from harm we may not even see. Even in the face of unknowns and uncertainties, God's protection reassures us that we are never left to face things on our own. His Spirit lives within us, guiding our decisions, comforting our hearts, and giving us courage to move forward in faith. When we trust in His protection, we learn to let go of fear and to rest in the confidence that God, who knows all things, is watching over us with love and care.

God's protection doesn't only cover our physical safety; it also guards our hearts and minds. He helps us to resist the lies, doubts, and fears that try to pull us away from His truth. When we feel tempted, discouraged, or attacked by thoughts that seek to weaken our faith, God's Word is a powerful shield, reminding us of His promises and giving us strength to stand firm. His truth is a barrier against the enemy's schemes, a fortress that surrounds us and keeps our minds at peace. He equips us with His Word, teaching us to hold onto His promises, to cling to His love, and to trust in His protection. When we meditate on His Word and let it fill our hearts, we are covered by a peace that cannot be shaken, a security that comes from knowing that our lives are in His hands.

God's protection is also a reminder of His constant presence. He is not a distant God who only watches from afar; He is near, surrounding us on every side. In times of trouble, He draws even closer, wrapping us in His loving arms and whispering words of comfort and reassurance. His protection is like a warm blanket on a cold night, a shelter in the storm, and a rock that holds firm when everything else seems uncertain. Knowing that God is encircling us allows us to walk through life with courage, for we are guarded by the One who created all things, who holds all power, and who loves us beyond measure. We are His precious children, and He has promised to keep us safe, to fight for us, and to protect us from harm.

When we are encircled by God's protection, we can face each day with peace, knowing that He sees everything we cannot. He is the God who watches over us while we sleep, who walks with us through every valley, and who celebrates with us on the mountaintops. His protection is a gift, a blessing that surrounds us wherever we go. Even when we face battles, trials, or fears, we are never abandoned. God is our constant companion, our shield, and our comfort. His protection assures us that He is in control, that no harm can reach us without passing through His loving hands, and that He is always working for our good, even when we can't see it.

God's protection also teaches us to trust Him more deeply. Each time we face a challenge and experience His care, our faith grows stronger. We learn to rely on Him, to rest in His promises, and to believe that He is always with us. His protection helps us to let go of worry, to surrender our fears, and to find comfort in His presence. As we trust in His protection, we find a peace that the world cannot give, a peace that comes from knowing that we are safe in His hands. Being encircled by His protection means that we can move forward boldly, knowing that He is our defender and that His love surrounds us on all sides.

Let us embrace this truth and live with the confidence that we are encircled by the Almighty's protection. May we remember that no matter what we face, we are held securely by the God who never fails, who fights for us, and who keeps us under His wings. His protection is our strength, our comfort, and our peace, a constant reminder that we are loved, valued, and guarded by our heavenly Father.

Chapter 27 - Empowered for Excellence

To be empowered for excellence means that God equips us to pursue the very best in everything we do, filling us with the strength, wisdom, and dedication needed to honor Him through our efforts. In Colossians 3:23, we read, "And whatsoever ye do, do it heartily, as to the Lord." This verse calls us to give our all, to work with a full heart, not just for human praise but to glorify God Himself. Being empowered for excellence means that every task, big or small, becomes an opportunity to reflect God's love and goodness. When we approach our work, studies, relationships, and daily responsibilities with the intention to honor Him, we invite His Spirit to guide and strengthen us, giving our best because we know that our lives are a testament to His grace. God doesn't expect perfection from us, but He calls us to do everything with a spirit of excellence, striving to reflect His character in all we do.

God empowers us with gifts, talents, and abilities uniquely suited to our purpose, and when we use these with diligence and commitment, we are showing our gratitude for all He has given us. Pursuing excellence is a way to say "thank you" to God, to show that we value the gifts He has entrusted to us. Excellence isn't about being the best compared to others; it's about being the best we can be, according to the potential God has placed within us. As we dedicate ourselves to our tasks, we invite God to work through us, making each effort a reflection of His creativity, wisdom, and strength. This commitment to excellence transforms the ordinary into something extraordinary, as even the simplest act done with love and dedication becomes an offering to God.

Excellence requires focus, perseverance, and a willing heart. God empowers us to keep going, even when the journey is hard, and to strive for greatness without becoming discouraged by setbacks. His Spirit within us gives us the patience to learn, the humility to grow, and the courage to try again when we stumble. Pursuing excellence is a journey, one that takes time, effort, and dedication, but God is with us in each step, shaping us and molding us to become more like Him. He provides us with the strength to overcome challenges, the wisdom to make good choices, and the passion to pursue our calling wholeheartedly. When we are empowered by God, we are equipped to face obstacles, to rise above difficulties, and to keep moving forward, knowing that He is our source of strength.

Being empowered for excellence also means striving to reflect God's love, kindness, and integrity in our interactions with others. Every word we speak, every decision we make, and every action we take can shine His light in the world. We are called to be examples of His love, showing compassion, patience, and respect to those around us. Pursuing excellence in our relationships means being honest, caring, and supportive, treating others as we would want to be treated, and seeking to encourage and uplift them. God empowers us to live with integrity, to do what is right, even when no one is watching, and to be faithful in all things. Our lives become a testimony to His goodness, a reflection of His love, and a message of hope for those who may not yet know Him.

God's empowerment helps us to find purpose and joy in our work, no matter how simple or complex the task may be. When we do everything as unto the Lord, we are reminded that each effort matters, each detail has value, and each moment is an opportunity to glorify God. Our work, whether it's at school, at home, or in our communities, becomes a way to honor God, as we give our best not for human recognition but to please our Heavenly Father. This perspective brings joy to our efforts, knowing that our work is a form of worship, a chance to use our gifts to serve others, and a way to contribute to God's kingdom. God's empowerment fills us with a sense of purpose, helping us to approach each day with gratitude, enthusiasm, and a willingness to make a difference.

As we strive for excellence, we grow in faith, character, and wisdom. God uses our commitment to excellence to shape us, to teach us, and to help us become more like Jesus. Each challenge we face, each success we celebrate, and each lesson we learn helps us to grow stronger, wiser, and more compassionate. God's empowerment gives us the resilience to keep going, the faith to trust in His plans, and the grace to find joy in the journey. We learn to rely on His strength, to seek His guidance, and to rest in His love. As we grow in excellence, we discover that it's not about achieving perfection but about giving our best and trusting God with the rest. He takes our efforts, no matter how small, and uses them for His glory, making each step of faith a part of His beautiful plan.

Pursuing excellence also inspires those around us, encouraging them to give their best and to seek God's purpose for their lives. When people see our dedication, integrity, and joy, they are drawn to the source of our strength—God Himself. Our commitment to excellence becomes a testimony of His love, a beacon of hope, and a reminder that God empowers all who seek Him. Each act of kindness, each word of encouragement, and each moment of hard work can plant seeds of faith in the hearts of others, showing them that a life lived for God is a life filled with meaning, purpose, and joy. We become examples of His love in action, witnesses to His grace, and vessels of His light, making an impact that goes beyond what we can see.

God's empowerment gives us the courage to pursue excellence, knowing that He has a plan for us and that He is with us every step of the way. We don't have to rely on our own strength because He is our source of wisdom, patience, and endurance. When we face obstacles, we can turn to Him, trusting that He will guide us, support us, and help us to overcome. His empowerment is a gift, a promise that we are not alone, and a reminder that with Him, all things are possible. As we lean on His strength, we find that we are able to accomplish more than we ever thought possible, achieving excellence not for our own glory but for His.

To be empowered for excellence is to live each day with purpose, joy, and a heart full of gratitude for the gifts God has given us. It's a call to do our best in every situation, to approach each task with enthusiasm, and to serve others with love and humility. When we pursue excellence, we are honoring God, using our lives to reflect His goodness and grace. Let us embrace this calling, striving for excellence in all we do, empowered by His love, strengthened by His Spirit, and guided by His truth.

Chapter 28 – Enlarged

To be enlarged by God means to have our hearts, our spirits, and our capacity to love, serve, and grow expanded in ways beyond our natural ability. In Isaiah 54:2, we read, "Enlarge the place of thy tent," which is an invitation from God to make room in our lives for His blessings, His love, and His purposes. This verse reminds us that God desires to stretch us, to help us reach new levels of faith, compassion, and strength as we follow Him. When God enlarges us, He gives us a greater ability to love others, even those who may be difficult to love, filling us with His love so that it overflows to those around us. He softens our hearts and helps us to see people as He sees them, with compassion, patience, and kindness. This enlargement of our hearts enables us to serve more selflessly, to forgive more freely, and to extend grace more abundantly, just as He does for us. God enlarges us to be more like Him, filling us with His Spirit so that we can be vessels of His love and light in the world.

As God enlarges our capacity to serve, He also increases our willingness and desire to make a difference in the lives of others. When our hearts are expanded by His love, we begin to see service not as an obligation but as a privilege. We feel a deep desire to help, to reach out, and to lift others up, knowing that we are part of God's plan to bless and encourage those around us. God equips us with the strength, patience, and wisdom we need to serve others well, giving us a heart that delights in doing good. Serving becomes a joy, a way of expressing our gratitude for all that God has done in our lives. He helps us to grow in humility, putting the needs of others before our own and showing love in action. As our capacity to serve grows, we find ourselves willing to step out of our comfort zones, to go the extra mile, and to offer our time, energy, and resources to bless those in need.

God's enlargement of our lives also means an increased capacity to grow spiritually. As He stretches us, He invites us to go deeper in our relationship with Him, to know Him more, and to trust Him more fully. Our faith is strengthened as we step out, rely on His promises, and experience His faithfulness in new ways. This growth often comes through challenges, as God uses difficult situations to build our character, to teach us patience, and to help us become more resilient. Each trial we face with faith expands our spiritual capacity, making us stronger and more able to handle future challenges with peace and confidence. God enlarges us to bear more fruit for His kingdom, to have a greater impact on the world around us, and to become a beacon of hope for others. This growth is not just for our benefit but for His glory, as our lives become a testimony of His power, love, and grace.

As we are enlarged, God gives us a greater vision for what is possible with Him. He helps us to dream bigger, to see beyond our limitations, and to believe that He can do exceedingly abundantly above all that we ask or think. Our minds and hearts are opened to the amazing possibilities of what God can do through us when we surrender our lives to Him. This enlarged vision fills us with hope, motivating us to keep going, to keep trusting, and to keep working for His kingdom. God invites us to expand our tent, to make room for the new things He wants to do in and through us. As we trust Him to enlarge our capacity, we begin to see how He can use our lives in ways we never imagined, blessing us so that we can be a blessing to others.

God's enlargement also brings a greater capacity for joy, peace, and contentment in Him. As He stretches our hearts and minds, we learn to find our satisfaction in His presence, to rest in His love, and to rejoice in His goodness. Our joy is no longer dependent on circumstances, but on the unchanging truth of God's love and faithfulness. We learn to be content in all situations, knowing that God is with us and that He is working all things together for our good. This enlarged heart is filled with gratitude, with praise, and with a peace that passes all understanding. We become more patient, more understanding, and more willing to wait on God's timing, trusting that He knows what is best for us. As our hearts grow, we are able to see God's hand in every part of our lives, and we are filled with a deep sense of gratitude for His constant presence and guidance.

Being enlarged by God means that we are continually being transformed, continually growing, and continually becoming more like Christ. This transformation is a journey, a process that requires us to be open, willing, and humble before God. He gently stretches us, helping us to let go of fears, doubts, and limitations that hold us back, and inviting us to walk in the fullness of His purpose. As we surrender to His will, we find ourselves being equipped and empowered for the plans He has for us. Our lives take on new meaning, and we find joy in every step, knowing that we are part of something bigger than ourselves. God's enlargement allows us to live fully, to love deeply, and to serve faithfully, as we become more and more like the person He created us to be.

God's call to enlarge the place of our tent is a call to faith, to trust Him to do in us what we cannot do on our own. He invites us to grow, to stretch, and to expand our lives so that we can contain more of His love, more of His Spirit, and more of His purpose. This enlargement is a blessing, a gift that enriches our lives and brings us closer to Him. As we open our hearts to God's work, we experience the joy of living a life that is filled with His presence, His power, and His peace. Let us embrace this enlargement, trusting that God will equip us, strengthen us, and guide us as we grow in love, in service, and in faith, for His glory and His kingdom.

Chapter 29 - Endued with Power

To be endued with power means to be filled with the strength, courage, and ability that comes from the Holy Spirit, equipping us to do God's work with confidence and purpose. In Luke 24:49, Jesus tells His followers, "Endued with power from on high," showing us that this power is not from our own strength but from God Himself. The Holy Spirit is given to us as a source of divine strength, guiding us, helping us, and empowering us to live boldly for Christ. When we are filled with the Holy Spirit, we find the courage to face challenges, the wisdom to make godly choices, and the passion to share God's love with others. Being endued with power means that we are never alone in our mission; God's Spirit lives within us, enabling us to carry out His will with a strength far greater than our own. The Spirit equips us to serve, to love, to forgive, and to witness to others about the hope we have in Christ. This power transforms our lives, giving us the ability to rise above fear, doubt, and weakness because we are fueled by God's strength.

God's Spirit within us gives us a deep, unshakable assurance that He is always with us, leading us and empowering us in every situation. The power of the Holy Spirit enables us to walk in faith, even when the path is uncertain. It fills us with a peace that cannot be shaken, a joy that goes beyond circumstances, and a love that reaches out to others. We find ourselves able to forgive where we once held onto bitterness, to show kindness where we once struggled with impatience, and to speak truth where we once might have been silent. This divine power makes us bold in our faith, confident in God's promises, and unafraid to stand for what is right. The Spirit fills us with the gifts needed to serve God's kingdom, whether in teaching, helping, encouraging, or leading. Being endued with power means that our lives are marked by God's presence, that His Spirit guides our words, our actions, and our choices, reflecting His love and purpose to everyone around us.

With the Holy Spirit's power, we are equipped to face trials and challenges that come our way. When life feels overwhelming, God's Spirit strengthens us, reminding us that we are not facing difficulties alone. His power is there to comfort us in sorrow, to give us peace in confusion, and to provide strength in weakness. No matter how hard things may seem, the Holy Spirit enables us to endure, to persevere, and to keep moving forward in faith. He lifts us up when we feel discouraged and fills us with hope when situations seem hopeless. This power from on high is a gift that sustains us, helping us to stay grounded in God's promises and to stand firm in our faith. We don't have to rely on our own limited abilities because God's Spirit is our helper, our guide, and our strength, working within us to accomplish things we could never do on our own.

Being endued with power also gives us a heart for serving others and sharing the Gospel. The Spirit stirs a passion within us to reach out, to show compassion, and to tell others about the love and salvation found in Jesus. He gives us the words to speak, the courage to share, and the wisdom to know when to act. When we are led by the Spirit, our lives become a testimony of God's grace, a living example of His love, and a beacon of hope for those who are lost. This power helps us to live with integrity, to act with kindness, and to speak with gentleness, reflecting Christ in everything we do. It gives us the boldness to stand firm in our beliefs, to resist temptation, and to hold fast to God's truth. We become vessels of His light in the world, channels of His peace, and instruments of His love, pointing others toward Him through our actions and our words.

This power from the Holy Spirit transforms us from the inside out, making us more like Christ each day. We become patient, kind, forgiving, and humble, not by our own effort but by the Spirit working within us. His power helps us to overcome weaknesses, to break free from old habits, and to walk in newness of life. It gives us a new perspective, helping us to see others with compassion, to serve without expecting anything in return, and to love without conditions. The Holy Spirit renews our minds, filling us with God's truth, and helping us to resist the lies of the world. This transformation is a journey, one that requires us to stay close to God, to seek His guidance, and to rely on His strength. As we yield to the Spirit, we grow in wisdom, grace, and faith, becoming the people God created us to be.

God's power through His Spirit also equips us to use our gifts for His glory. Each of us has been given unique abilities and talents, and the Spirit empowers us to use them to bless others and build up His kingdom. Whether in teaching, hospitality, music, prayer, or service, the Holy Spirit enables us to make a difference, to bring hope, and to inspire others. When we offer our gifts to God, His Spirit multiplies our efforts, making our work fruitful and impactful. We are able to do more than we ever imagined because we are not working in our own strength; we are working in the power of God. This empowerment gives us confidence, knowing that our efforts are not in vain and that God is using our lives to accomplish His purposes. As we serve, we experience the joy of being part of something greater, a mission that has eternal significance and a purpose that fulfills our deepest desires.

The power of the Holy Spirit also fills us with hope and resilience. We know that God is always with us, that His Spirit is our constant companion, and that His power within us will never fade. This hope gives us the strength to keep going, even when the road is rough, and to trust that God is working all things together for our good. Being endued with power means that we can face the unknown with confidence, knowing that God has already gone before us and prepared the way. It reminds us that we are not defined by our weaknesses but by His strength, that we are not limited by our fears but empowered by His love. With the Holy Spirit, we can walk boldly, live joyfully, and trust completely, knowing that God's power will sustain us through every season of life.

As we live empowered by the Spirit, we become vessels of His grace, His mercy, and His truth. Our lives become a witness to His love, a testimony of His faithfulness, and a reflection of His glory. The Spirit fills us with compassion, helping us to reach out to the hurting, to comfort the brokenhearted, and to encourage the weary. We are empowered to be peacemakers, to bring joy, and to be a source of strength for others. This power is not for our own glory but for God's, enabling us to fulfill His purpose and to show the world His love. Being endued with power from on high is a gift, a blessing, and a call to live fully for God, letting His Spirit guide us, strengthen us, and fill us with His love every step of the way.

Chapter 30 - Entrusted with Influence

To be entrusted with influence means that God has given us the power to positively impact the lives of others, to bring hope, to uplift, and to reflect His love in a way that draws people closer to Him. In Matthew 5:13, Jesus says, "Ye are the salt of the earth," highlighting our role in the world as people who can make a difference, add value, and bring goodness wherever we go. Just as salt preserves, flavors, and enhances, we are called to bring out the best in others, to encourage, to inspire, and to make life richer for those around us. Being entrusted with influence is a gift and a responsibility from God, asking us to use our words, actions, and attitudes to bring His light into every situation. Influence is not about power or control; it's about love, compassion, and setting an example that reflects God's heart. Through our influence, we have the opportunity to show others what it means to live a life of faith, to walk in kindness, and to embrace hope even in difficult times.

God calls us to be people who lift others up, who bring encouragement, and who help others see the goodness in life. Being the salt of the earth means that we bring flavor and joy, showing the world the beauty of God's love and the peace that comes from knowing Him. Our influence can have a lasting impact, as our words and actions leave an impression that others carry with them. When we show kindness, when we are patient, when we forgive, and when we love unconditionally, we are using our influence to plant seeds of faith and hope in the lives of others. God has entrusted us with this influence to be a blessing, to bring healing, and to help others find their own purpose and identity in Christ. As we live out our faith, we become a testimony of His grace, showing others that there is a way of life that leads to peace, joy, and fulfillment.

Being entrusted with influence means being intentional about how we live and interact with others. Each word we speak, each decision we make, and each way we respond to challenges can impact those around us, either for good or for harm. God wants us to use this influence to guide others toward Him, to help them see His love through our actions, and to inspire them to seek His presence in their own lives. Influence is like a ripple in a pond; one act of kindness, one moment of patience, or one word of encouragement can spread and create a positive effect far beyond what we can see. God uses our influence as a tool to reach others, to show them His goodness, and to reveal His truth in ways that touch the heart. When we live as the salt of the earth, we bring preservation and life, helping others to hold onto hope and to stay strong in their own faith.

Influence also means living with integrity, showing others what it means to be honest, faithful, and true to God's Word. When we live with integrity, people see that our faith is genuine, that our love is sincere, and that our trust in God is real. This kind of influence speaks louder than words, showing others that our relationship with God affects every part of our lives. God has entrusted us with the power to be role models, to be examples of what it means to live a life that honors Him. We are not perfect, but as we strive to walk in God's ways, we inspire others to do the same, encouraging them to seek a closer relationship with Him. Influence is not about being in the spotlight; it's about letting our lives point to Jesus, so that others may see Him in us and be drawn to His love.

As salt of the earth, we are called to stand out, to live differently, and to bring hope to a world that often feels lost and uncertain. God has given us the power to influence others not for our own glory, but to reflect His goodness and to spread His message of salvation. This influence is a privilege, an opportunity to touch lives and to make a positive difference. Each day, we have the chance to encourage someone, to offer a helping hand, or to be a voice of comfort. God uses our influence to work through us, to reach people who may be struggling, lonely, or searching for meaning. When we live with love, when we treat others with respect, and when we show compassion, we are using our influence to point others to God's unchanging love.

Being entrusted with influence also calls us to be mindful and humble, to use this gift wisely and responsibly. God wants us to be aware of the impact we have, to recognize the ways our words and actions can affect others, and to choose kindness, patience, and understanding. Influence means having the power to shape others' thoughts, feelings, and even their faith journeys. God wants us to use this power with love, to be careful not to harm others but to encourage them, to help them grow, and to be a source of support. Our influence is a reflection of God's influence on us, as His Spirit works in our hearts, changing us and helping us to live in a way that brings glory to Him. We are His representatives, His ambassadors, and through our influence, we carry His message of hope, love, and grace to the world.

God has given us influence as a tool for building His kingdom, for making a difference that reaches beyond ourselves. This influence is not for our own gain, but for His purpose, to be used in ways that bless others and draw them closer to Him. When we remember that our influence comes from God, we begin to see each interaction, each relationship, and each opportunity as a chance to serve Him. We become mindful of the example we set, understanding that people are watching how we live and learning from how we respond to life's challenges. By staying close to God, by relying on His wisdom, and by allowing His Spirit to guide us, we use our influence in a way that honors Him and impacts others for good.

Living as the salt of the earth means that we are constantly growing, learning, and seeking to become more like Christ. As God shapes us, as He strengthens our faith, and as He fills us with His love, our influence becomes a light that shines in the darkness. People are drawn to the peace, the joy, and the hope that we have, and through our influence, they begin to see God's love for themselves. Being entrusted with influence is a responsibility, but it is also a blessing, a chance to be a part of God's work in the world. Each time we choose kindness, each time we offer forgiveness, and each time we show compassion, we are using our influence to plant seeds of faith in others' hearts.

Let us embrace this calling to be the salt of the earth, to use our influence for good, and to make a difference that honors God. May we live each day with purpose, knowing that our actions, our words, and our choices have the power to impact others. As we walk in God's ways, as we trust in His guidance, and as we show His love, our influence becomes a powerful tool in His hands, spreading His light, His hope, and His peace to all we meet.

Chapter 31 - Enabled to Encourage

To be enabled to encourage means that God has equipped us with the power and wisdom to lift others up, to offer hope, and to support them in their walk of faith. In 1 Thessalonians 5:11, we are reminded, "Wherefore comfort yourselves together, and edify one another," calling us to be a source of strength and encouragement to those around us. Encouragement is a gift from God, a way to share His love and to remind others that they are not alone in their struggles. When we encourage others, we are doing more than just offering kind words; we are bringing comfort, support, and strength that comes from God Himself. Being enabled to encourage means that God has placed within us the ability to see the needs of others, to listen to their burdens, and to speak words of life and hope. It's a powerful way to serve, as our words and actions can make a lasting impact on someone's heart, giving them the courage to keep going, the strength to face challenges, and the assurance that God is with them.

Encouragement is essential for our faith journey, as we all face times when we feel weary, uncertain, or discouraged. God calls us to be there for each other, to provide the support and love that help us stay strong in our faith. When we encourage others, we remind them of God's promises, helping them to see that He is faithful, that He is working in their lives, and that He will never leave them. Encouragement helps us to stay focused on God's goodness, even in difficult times, and to trust that He has a purpose for everything we go through. We are enabled by God to bring this encouragement to others, to be a source of hope and strength, especially when they are feeling weak or lost. By lifting others up, we are fulfilling God's command to love and serve, showing them that they are valued, cared for, and loved by Him.

Being enabled to encourage also means being willing to listen, to offer a shoulder to lean on, and to stand alongside others in their times of need.

Encouragement is not just about speaking; it's about being present, showing compassion, and letting others know that they are not alone. Sometimes, the simple act of being there for someone, praying with them, or just listening to their concerns can bring more comfort than words alone. God empowers us to be that steady presence, to be a friend and a supporter, to help others find peace in knowing that they are surrounded by love and understanding. Our encouragement helps to build others up, to strengthen their faith, and to remind them that God is with them every step of the way. When we walk alongside others, we are a reflection of God's love, a reminder that He is present in every situation.

Encouragement also gives us the chance to share our own experiences and testimonies of God's faithfulness. When we have been through challenges, struggles, or doubts, and have seen God's hand at work, we can use those experiences to uplift others who may be going through similar situations. By sharing how God has helped us, we give others the hope that He will do the same for them. Our testimonies become powerful tools of encouragement, showing others that they too can overcome, that they too can find strength in God, and that they too can trust Him with all their hearts. God uses our lives, our stories, and our experiences to bring encouragement to others, to help them see that they are not alone, and to remind them that God's grace is always sufficient.

Encouragement is a way to build unity within the body of Christ, to strengthen our relationships with each other, and to create a community of love and support. When we encourage one another, we are fulfilling the purpose God has for His church, to be a family that supports, uplifts, and cares for each other. Each word of encouragement helps to bring us closer together, to form bonds of trust, and to create a strong foundation of faith. As we encourage each other, we grow together, learning to rely on God and on each other, building a community that reflects His love. This unity is a powerful testimony to the world, showing others that there is a place where they can find hope, love, and support, where they are welcomed and valued. Our encouragement helps to build this community, to create a safe place where people can grow in their faith and find comfort in times of need.

God enables us to encourage others through His Spirit, giving us the words, the wisdom, and the compassion we need to lift others up. We don't have to rely on our own strength because God fills us with His love, helping us to see others as He sees them. He gives us a heart that cares, a mind that understands, and a spirit that is willing to serve. Through His Spirit, we are empowered to bring encouragement that truly touches hearts, that brings comfort and peace, and that helps others to see God's love in a real and personal way. When we pray, when we seek God's guidance, and when we ask for His help, He gives us the ability to be a light for others, to speak words that heal, and to offer support that strengthens.

Encouragement is also a way for us to grow in our own faith, as we see God working through us to bless others. Each time we encourage someone, we are reminded of God's goodness, His faithfulness, and His power. We see how He uses us to make a difference, to bring hope, and to show His love. This builds our faith, helping us to trust Him more, to rely on His strength, and to be more willing to serve. As we encourage others, we become more like Christ, learning to love as He loves, to give as He gives, and to care as He cares. Encouragement is a blessing, a gift from God that enriches our lives, that strengthens our relationships, and that brings us closer to Him.

God has enabled us to be encouragers, to be people who lift others up, who speak life, and who bring hope. Let us embrace this calling, knowing that each word, each action, and each moment of support has the power to change lives, to bring healing, and to strengthen faith. Let us be faithful in encouraging one another, in comforting each other, and in building each other up, as we walk together in faith, trusting in God's promises and relying on His love.

Conclusion

As we come to the end of "Enabled: Living God's Purpose With Power," let us remember that this journey of faith is ongoing and God's power in us is not limited to a moment—it's meant to carry us through every day of our lives. Throughout this book, we've explored how God equips, strengthens, and empowers each of us to live out His calling, reflecting His love, truth, and purpose. Being enabled by God is not just about having moments of strength or insight; it's about letting His Spirit fill us daily, guiding our steps, and sustaining us in all we do. The Christian life is a continuous walk of trusting and depending on God, even when challenges arise. There will be days when we feel weak, days when we face obstacles or moments of doubt, but these are the times when God's power becomes most evident. As Paul wrote in 2 Corinthians 12:9, "My grace is sufficient for thee: for my strength is made perfect in weakness." God enables us in our weaknesses, and His grace is the foundation that supports us, allowing us to press on with courage and hope.

Living enabled by God's purpose and power means making a daily commitment to rely on Him, to draw from His wisdom, and to walk in obedience to His Word. We are called to live intentionally, to use the gifts He has given us, and to encourage others along the way. Every day brings new opportunities to live for God, to make choices that honor Him, and to show His love to the world. This life of being enabled by God is one of continuous growth, where we learn more about His character, His love, and His will for our lives. The Holy Spirit is our constant companion, always ready to guide, comfort, and empower us. We do not walk alone; God's Spirit is within us, enabling us to be bold, to stand firm in our faith, and to face whatever comes with peace. Our mission, as followers of Christ, is to keep moving forward, to keep sharing the message of hope, and to keep growing in love and service.

As you close this book, remember that God's enabling power is not only for extraordinary moments but also for the everyday. He is with you in the simple tasks, in the quiet acts of kindness, and in the unseen choices that reflect His goodness. Being enabled by God means that our lives are a testimony of His grace and power, even in small things. So continue to seek Him, to lean into His strength, and to trust that He is working in and through you for His glory. No matter where life takes you, know that you are enabled, strengthened, and supported by a God who never fails. Keep living with purpose, keep growing in faith, and let God's power be your guide as you walk in His purpose each day. You are empowered to live fully for Him, equipped to make a difference, and strengthened to fulfill the calling He has placed on your life. As you go forward, remember: God's power is within you, and with Him, you are truly enabled to live with courage, love, and unwavering faith.

Don't miss out!

Visit the website below and you can sign up to receive emails whenever Joshua Rhoades publishes a new book. There's no charge and no obligation.

https://books2read.com/r/B-A-AJLBB-IJEHF

BOOKS 2 READ

Connecting independent readers to independent writers.

Did you love *Enabled- Living God's Purpose With Power*? Then you should read *Unshakeable Faith- 31 Days of Peace in God's Word*[1] by Joshua Rhoades!

"Unshakeable Faith - 31 Days of Peace in God's Word" is a heartfelt devotional designed to guide readers through 31 days of discovering the unwavering peace that comes from trusting in God's promises. In a world filled with uncertainty, challenges, and personal struggles, many are searching for a peace that cannot be shaken. This book offers a comforting journey through Scripture, showing how, even in the darkest valleys or the most turbulent storms, God's love and guidance remain steadfast, inviting us to experience a peace beyond what the world can provide.

Each day in "Unshakeable Faith" is crafted to lead readers to a fresh, encouraging truth from God's Word that reminds them of His unwavering presence. These daily reflections aren't just brief moments of inspiration; they are meant to be a foundation of faith, equipping readers to stand firm no matter what they face. In each devotion, readers are invited to reflect, pray, and renew

---

1. https://books2read.com/u/49RB8W

2. https://books2read.com/u/49RB8W

their commitment to walking closely with God, letting His promises guide them. With verses chosen for their relevance to our lives today, this devotional brings readers into the heart of God's love and peace, even when life feels chaotic. Whether it's through words of Jesus that call us to trust or promises from the Psalms that show God's protective care, every devotion speaks to the timeless truth that God is our anchor, our refuge, and our peace.

One of the unique aspects of "Unshakeable Faith" is that it isn't just for those going through immediate trials; it's for anyone who wants to cultivate a life of deep-rooted peace and security in God. Day by day, this devotional builds up the reader's confidence in God's faithfulness, helping them develop a lasting, unshakeable faith that can stand the test of time. We live in times where anxiety, fear, and uncertainty often feel overwhelming. But with each day spent in God's Word, this book reminds us that true peace doesn't depend on our circumstances but on the One who controls them. Through stories of people from Scripture who trusted God's guidance, even when they couldn't see the full picture, "Unshakeable Faith" shows readers that peace is not only possible but is a promise we can hold onto.

The devotionals included are accessible, meaningful, and designed to resonate with those of any age or spiritual background who are seeking the stability that only God provides. Each day combines reflection and actionable steps so readers can take what they've learned and apply it to their lives immediately, building their trust and reliance on God. Alongside each devotion, reflective questions help readers delve deeper, making the experience personal and transformative. These questions encourage readers to explore how God's peace is at work in their own lives and how they can respond to His love, ultimately helping them to grow a faith that feels secure and close.

"Unshakeable Faith - 31 Days of Peace in God's Word" invites readers to lay down their anxieties, to trust in God's character, and to let His Word be the anchor that holds them steady. It is a book that meets readers in their real-life struggles, gently guiding them to the peace that only God can give, and encouraging them to live with an assurance that is grounded in His promises. Whether the reader is new to faith or has walked with God for many years, this devotional serves as a reminder that God's love is faithful, His peace is real, and His Word is the foundation upon which we can build a life of strength, joy, and unwavering hope.